D0561312

MEDITATIONS FOR
THE CREATIVE SPIRIT

The Art of the Soul

JOY SAWYER

BROADMAN
& HOLMAN
PUBLISHERS

Nashville, Tennessee

0-8054–1851–2

Published by Broadman & Holman Publishers, Nashville, Tennessee

Dewey Decimal Classification: 242
Subject Heading: DEVOTIONAL EXERCISES / THE ARTS

Scripture quotations marked The Message are from *The Message,* the New
Testament in Contemporary English, © 1993 by Eugene H. Peterson,
published by NavPress, Colorado Springs, Colo. Scripture quotations
marked NIV are from the Holy Bible, New International Version, copy-
right © 1973, 1978, 1984 by International Bible Society. Scripture quotations marked NASB are from the New American Standard Bible, © the
Lockman Foundation, 1960, 1962, 1963, 1968, 1971, 1972, 1973,
1975, 1977; used by permission.

Library of Congress Cataloging-in-Publication Data

Sawyer, Joy.
  The art of the soul : meditations for the creative spirit / Joy
Sawyer.
    p. cm.
  ISBN 0–8054–1851–2 (pb)
  1. Christian literature—Authorship—Meditations. I. Title.

BR44.S28 2000
242 68—dc21

99–057351
CIP

1 2 3 4 5 04 03 02 01 00

TO ANTON MARCO

for twenty-two years
of nourishing this
grateful art-beggar

Not deep the poet sees, but wide.

—MATTHEW ARNOLD

Contents

irst, this book is written with love for that church "taller than cathedral stone": those family, friends, and acquaintances who, over the years, shared their struggles (or lack thereof) concerning faith and art. There are several of us who had church frequently . . . over coffee, lunch, or dinner (rarely breakfast, of course), on the phone, through letters and e-mails, on noisy subways and quiet park benches, at movie theaters and HoJo's, in living rooms, dorm rooms, and cramped office cubicles. And it's especially for those who made me laugh.

So thank you for inviting me into such sacred ground in your souls, Rachelle, Cristal, Scott, Mary, Heather, Shannon, Todd, Jeff, Diane, Judith, Pete, Lausanne, Paula, Peter, Eric, Karen and Terry, Stephanie and Jon, Kristy and Doug, Tim and Susan, Kurt and Asha, Shari and Dave, Brooke and Craig, Chuck and Katie, John and Gail, Betsey and Brian, Brad and Nancy, Jeff and Olivia, Michael and Hallie, Bruce and Pippa, Mark and Tara, Elvie, Mark, Joe, Tom, Tony, Cynthia, Bill, Steve, Amy, Carmen, Cindy, Curt, Lydia, Susan, Barb, Roland, Don, Julia, Laura, Catherine, Shari, Danielle, Karen, Jo, Sanne, David, Chris, Lisa, Nancy, Anne, Sue, Judith, Randy, Heidi, Anthony, Doug, Brent, Barry, Bruce. No love, no time, no place, no conversation is ever wasted. This is for you and your art—with all my heart.

A faithful man of God, Ray Koterba, and his family in Rock Hill, South Carolina, first taught me to love and pursue the Jesus of the Scriptures. Thank you, Koterbas, for your example across the miles and years.

I'm deeply grateful to Leonard Goss, my editor at Broadman and Holman, a man of integrity and vision. He's made writing this book a true pleasure.

Lastly, I thank God for my husband, Scotty, an extraordinary artist of the soul. Thank you for loving the Art so passionately, no matter what our circumstances. That's the greatest gift in any marriage, love of mine—and it puts my best dreams to shame.

So You're Not Creative?
or Even If You Are, Let's Take
a Creative Road Trip

> *Creativity involves breaking out of established*
> *patterns in order to look at things in a different way.*
>
> —EDWARD DEBONO

I'm not one of those creative types."

If that's you talking, then perhaps a first, courageous step toward living the creative life is what Edward DeBono advocates above: breaking out of that well-worn, concrete-cerebrum-and-hardened-heart highway of thinking that you're not creative. Since God is creative, and you're made in the image of God, it's a natural, logical deduction that you're creative too. So let's expose that rugged rut for what it is: a bog-in-the-mud lie, designed to ruin your road trip through this life. No use spinning your wheels over a falsely foregone conclusion.

Or perhaps your rut is a different one. Say you're already convinced that you're one of those artistic types—but the terrain you've navigated so far is too predictable, too familiar. Maybe it would be fun to veer off the well-worn roads of your favorite creative territory and take a scenic spiritual side trip.

Anything can happen when you're riding in the royal blue Rambler of the Spirit.

After all, we're talking about riding shotgun with the same raucous God who flung bright, rolling stars down the dark bowling alley of the night and said, "Hey—this is good." The same elegant God who stopped for dinner one day and graciously spread the table of the heavens—the sparkling crystal bowl of sun, the silver-slivered spoon of moon. Not to mention the main dinner course of the earth. For that, he set out his best China.

The great thing about God-as-travel agent is that, no matter who you are or where you've been, he's always got something bigger up his timeless sleeve.

Endless creativity.

You're made in the image of the God who says to us in Ephesians 2:10 that "we are his workmanship"—his work of art. Another translation: We are his *poiema*—his very own handwritten Shakespearean sonnet. You're made in the image of the God who can take the disjointed words you've written and make beautiful (literary interpretation: imperfect and heartfelt) lyrics out of your life. You're made in the image of the God who can change the cynical soul's dirty diapers into the clean linens of a fresh, wonder-filled heart. You're made in the image of the God who can take your paper-clip string of both real and imagined failures—and actually transform them into something useful in the bustling office of your everyday life.

So let's kick those rusted prison doors of lies wide open, shall we? Creativity doesn't just belong to the painters, the poets, the musicians. It belongs to the Wednesday night bowlers, the nursery school teachers, the housewives who dish up tuna fish casserole. It belongs to the amateur verse scrawlers, the faithful letter writers, the moms who change diapers day after day, the office manager who knows when a pile of disheveled papers needs either a surge of genius or an out basket.

And this same creative God—the God of the 7-10 bowling split, smelly diapers, waste baskets—has a wild and wonderful purpose for the use of your creativity in this world. But you're probably going to need to take some risks in order to discover new scenic overlooks, new roadside diners. Good-bye, comfort zones of complacency.

Hello, frontiers of freedom.

So let's begin the road trip by imagining your heart is like a map of the United States. If you still don't think you're creative, here's an analogy: You've probably spent way too long tinkering with your computer in Utah—and the most sacrificial thing you could do right now is pack up your tidily-folded Bible verses and head to Florida for some sun. For some fun, even.

Or, if you're an artistic type, maybe you've squandered your time in kitschy-but-lucrative Vegas or moodily cloistered yourself away from the rest of us in a spiritually smoky Greenwich Village coffee shop. Time to come out and be a real artist. Time to come out and breathe some fresh air. Who knows? Maybe your heart could benefit from the good, old ordinary meatloaf and mashed potatoes of the Word.

You may not know what direction you're heading with this spiritual journey into creativity, but that's really OK. As the novelist E. L. Doctorow says, "[Creativity] is like driving a car at night. You can never see further than your headlights, but you can make the whole trip that way."

In this case, just follow the telltale taillights of the Artist-in-residence.

CREATIVE EXERCISE: *Make a detailed list of your creative struggles, questions, roadblocks. Don't hold back . . . try to get every one of them that you can on paper.*

SEND IN THE CLOWNS

Creativity is inventing,
experimenting, growing, taking risks,
breaking rules, making mistakes, and having fun.

—MARY LOU COOK

What are your obstacles to creativity—those problems that plop down smack in the middle of your three-ring-circus life like determined elephants? For some, it's the loud, ringmaster voice of self-doubt. As one artist friend confides, "I think if I claim to be an artist, I'll be required to be great at what I do. I often feel like I'm able to do a lot or want to do a lot—but I don't feel good at any one thing." Comparisons to other artists may also enter this arena: "I have friends whom I consider to be true artists," one writer says. "I'm afraid I'll be compared to them and be found wanting."

Yet another asks, "I always question the validity of my experience. Was it really real? How would others view that same experience?" For this artist, even the *life* that informs her art is a looming suspect on stilts.

Many other artists are concerned with walking the tightrope of time constraints. "The only time I have to write is when my children are taking naps," laments one woman. "How can I create what I want to create in such a short amount of time?"

As our friends in the land of Oz shivered so long ago, "Lions and tigers and bears . . ."

Oh my.

There are plenty of roaring obstacles to fear. Or are they really obstacles?

Circuses are chock-full of honking horns, bright colors, trapeze dangers, stinky animals, obnoxious clowns, crying babies, cotton candy, and toffee-coated peanuts. And there's the further distraction of three separate rings waging war for our undivided attention. Yet there is a lot that a circus can show us about what it means to be an artist.

It's the nature of a circus that, if you don't know what you're watching, you might think it's just a distraction, a grand conspiracy for your attention. Well, it is—in the best sense possible. You go to a circus to be entertained. You go to a circus to be awed by death-defying feats. And, even if you're eighty years old, you go to a circus . . . as a kid.

Do you remember at all what it was like to color in a coloring book? Arrange your green plastic Army men in neat, orderly rows and give them all good, old-fashioned American names? Braid your girlfriends' hair with plastic beads? Play air-guitar like Eric Clapton? If you can access just one memory of the slightest hint of creativity as a child, you're well on your way.

In order to frog-leap over your obstacles—real or imagined—art first needs to become what it was to you when you were young: *fun*. Later, you can get to the serious stuff: the discipline, the study. But for now, art doesn't mean you have to be the best still-life painter in the class. (That didn't stop you from hanging your early finger-paint masterpieces on the refrigerator, did it?) Or figure out what art form you need to focus on (hey, as a kid, you tried them all out, right?). Or even have a huge chunk of time to create. (Be honest: How much time did it take for you to use your creativity for under-the-bed storage when you were supposed to clean your room? Five minutes? Three?)

To begin to step around those pink elephants in your way, think *circus*. Think bright lights and wild colors and stomach-lurching, scary trapeze acts. Think that all the bright-light artists you know (whom you think are better than you), all the wild-color art forms you want to try (with seemingly no goal in mind), all the acts of car-pooling and daytimering (that seem to consume your life) aren't distractions. They are a normal part of being an artist. You're not supposed to get rid of them. They're meant to lead you to *the fun of art*.

So what if you have twenty minutes a day to write? I once heard the story of a woman novelist with eight children who wrote a book in a year—during the time *she spent on the toilet*. What if Barbra Streisand (or your next door neighbor) sings better than you do? Isn't it thrilling to hear those glass-shattering high notes—music that inspires you to offer your song in the world as well?

As to the validity of your experience—well, *you* are the only one under the circus tent who has your particular seat, your particular perspective. No one else sees the dancing bears quite the way you do.

So, to start living as an artist—and as an artist of the soul—you might want to begin as you did in the beginning: as a kid. With a childlike spirit. Ready for fun.

Try sending in the clowns.

SCRIPTURE MEDITATION: [*Jesus said,*] *"I'm telling you, once and for all, that unless you return to square one and start over like children, you're not even going to get a look at the kingdom, let alone get in. Whoever becomes simple and elemental again, like this child, will rank high in God's kingdom. What's more, when you receive the childlike on my account, it's the same as receiving me"* (Matt. 18:2–5 *The Message*).

ART? WHAT A WASTE . . .

*There are worse crimes than
burning books. One of them is not reading them.*

—JOSEPH BRODSKY

The former poet laureate of the United States, Joseph Brodsky, grew up amidst Russian cultural and intellectual oppression. Brodsky was thirteen the day he and his classmates were corralled into an auditorium and ordered to fall to their knees and mourn the death of Joseph Stalin. "Weep, children, weep!" a stern woman cried from the front of the room. "As for me," Brodsky recalls, "I did not weep."

The young poet's first act of resistance was a literary harbinger of things to come: He survived years of prison cells and mental hospitals for the dubious crime of thinking independently. Even though Brodsky's first arrest came because he wrote poetry, his fellow Russian writers were enthusiastic about his work, albeit quietly. In those days, literature was shared through what is called "Samizdat publication." A person who reads something he likes makes five copies, passes on the original to another person, who then makes his five copies as well, and so on. In this way, the country's literature was disseminated underground.

It was through the Samizdat method that Brodsky first encountered what he felt was the finest manuscript he'd ever read. While visiting a friend, Brodsky watched the man unearth a metal box in his backyard—and gingerly pull out a copy of a book that would change Brodsky's life forever: Alexander Solzhenitsyn's *Gulag Archipelago*. Solzhenitsyn's realistic, compelling documentary of Russian life fueled Brodsky's determination, at age nineteen, to pursue fervently the literary life he'd chosen.

When the writer and critic Malcolm Muggeridge was asked about Solzhenitsyn's writing, the journalist pointed out the irony that the man he thought of as "the most perceptive Christian of this century" emerged from intense religious persecution. How did Solzhenitsyn know so much about Christianity in a culture so hostile toward religion? Muggeridge answers that he believes Alexander Solzhenitsyn was tutored in the school of faith . . . through the novels of Leo Tolstoy.

Leo Tolstoy . . . to Alexander Solzhenitsyn . . . to Joseph Brodsky. The combination is to literature what "Tinker-to-Evers-to-Chance" once was to baseball. The three bases of fiction, nonfiction, and poetry are thoroughly covered through this literary triple play: One person's writing connects with another's life—who, in turn, writes something that connects with yet another person's life. The cycle is strikingly clear. And Tolstoy, who spent much of his life severely depressed, probably had no idea his work would carry such lasting literary impact—not only on his readers, but also on those who, like Solzhenitsyn, were both readers *and* writers.

The words of this storyteller hit home with others in a way he never could have envisioned.

A similar story is recounted in the Bible. In Mark 14, we read about a very bold and splashy woman (in another portion of Scripture, she is identified as a prostitute) who crashes a moral-majority party. She pours her most expensive perfume over Jesus' head as a special gift—and the supper-club guests are furious. You can imagine the scene: A disreputable woman bursts through the front door wearing her fuschia lipstick and clingy nylon dress, while the rest of the guests, dressed in neat khakis and polo shirts, get royally steamed as they nibble wontons. That perfume could have been sold for a year's wages, they fume. It might have funded important ministry activities!

But Jesus *loves* this woman's brazen love. In fact, he tells the indignant group that he imagines wherever in the world his story is told, the story of her wasted perfume would also be "talked about admiringly." "She did what she could *when* she could," Jesus marvels (see *The Message*). It was exactly the right thing—at the right time. She was in tune with the player who had perfect pitch.

Some people may tell you that writing novels is a waste of your time—and God's. That the hours spent practicing stand-up comedy routines are better spent volunteering for the soup kitchen. But the real question is not *what* we're doing, but the art of *how* we're doing it. Do we do "what we can, when we can"? In other words, are we pouring out the most costly essence of our souls on the person of Christ? If so, he will live in and through our lives. We share the joy of knowing the story of our "wasted lives" will definitely *not* be wasted.

Just as the woman in Mark 14 had no idea we'd be talking admiringly about her story right now, *today*—and Leo Tolstoy had no clue his words would one day shape the religious sensibilities of Alexander Solzhenitsyn—so Solzenitsyn didn't know that one day a young, teenage poet named Joseph Brodsky would read the *Gulag*—and grow up to be named the Poet Laureate of the United States.

We are God's living Samizdats—handed carefully in this world from person to person, in order that the Story might be told again and again, in a million different ways.

The art of the soul. What a waste it is.

SCRIPTURE MEDITATION: *The disciples came up and asked [Jesus], "Why do you tell stories?" He replied, "You've been given insight into God's kingdom. You know how it works. Not everybody has this gift, this insight; it hasn't been given to them. Whenever someone has a ready heart for this, the insights and understandings flow freely. But if there is no readiness, any trace of receptivity soon disappears. That's why I tell stories: to create readiness, to nudge the people toward receptive insight"* (Matt. 13:10–13 *The Message*).

4

Einstein's Genius

*Genius is the ability to
reduce the complicated to the simple.*

—C. W. CERAN

The author Jerome Weidman recounts an unusual musical experience he had at a New York dinner party. After the meal, the guests were led into the drawing room, where it became obvious by the assembled instruments that the evening's entertainment was chamber music.

Weidman claims to be tone deaf, so when he took his seat, he immediately retreated into his own private world of thoughts. To him, music was simply an "arrangement of noises," as he called it, and he'd already chalked up the evening to a night of polite boredom.

After some time, he became aware of people applauding. Then someone to his right asked him if he liked Bach. As Weidman turned to answer, he immediately recognized the unruly shock of white hair. The voice belonged to Albert Einstein.

As the two conversed, Weidman admitted his lack of knowledge of Bach, as well as of any musical subject. Einstein then insisted that Weidman leave the concert with him, and led him upstairs to a book-filled study. How long have you felt this way about music, Einstein quizzed him. Is there any music you like?

Weidman sheepishly admitted that he was partial to Bing Crosby.

Einstein seemed pleased. He pulled out a record album and played a Crosby song. Then he asked Weidman what he'd just heard.

What followed was an object lesson in life. As Weidman clumsily sang back to Einstein what he'd heard, the scientist was delighted. He exclaimed that Weidman could, indeed, hear music—and that what he'd just done was a study in natural law. Einstein noted that when Weidman first learned arithmetic as an elementary student, had he been forced to do long division he would have panicked. And he probably would have remained convinced he couldn't do it, perhaps for the rest of his life.

But, Einstein went on to say, if he'd been able to start with elementary skills and then work his way up, he soon would have encountered long division—and have mastered it. What Einstein was saying was simple: Let's begin with the elementaries of Bing Crosby, and continue from there.

The scientist continued the lesson by playing a variety of songs on the phonograph. After Weidman listened to several and sang back the melody lines, Einstein smiled broadly. "Now we are ready for Bach!" he exclaimed triumphantly. The two went downstairs and returned to the evening's entertainment.

After the concert, as the hostess of the evening glared at Weidman, she apologized profusely to Einstein for his missing so much of the musical performance. The scientist gave his apologies as well, but then patiently explained that he and his new friend "were engaged in the greatest activity of which man is capable." When the hostess asked him what that was, Einstein simply smiled and put his arm around Weidman.

"Opening up yet another fragment of the frontier of beauty," he said.

The genius of the universe, Jesus Christ, begins the study of his music where we can begin. "In the beginning was the Word," John says, "and the Word was with God, and the Word was God. He was with God in the beginning" (John 1:1–2 NIV). In Jesus' own story, God begins with one Word. And that is the same Word where our story, our song, our poem begins—at the beginning.

Oftentimes, as we create, we may feel overwhelmed by the sheer magnitude of tackling our "Bachs"—our complicated, large artistic projects. But to regain perspective, all we need to do is to remember to begin with Bing Crosby. To begin with one sentence, one melody line, a few lines of a pencil drawing. Such are the fragments where the frontier of beauty begins.

The same principle is at work spiritually. Many of us panic because we're convinced we must begin somewhere other than the beginning. We start with what we *think* a Christian should do and say and be—trying to be good, to be moral—rather than learning the rhythms and sounds of the music, note by simple note, and growing into the beauty of more difficult spiritual passages. We think we're spiritually deaf, rather than the fact that we're unskilled in the rudimentaries of the faith. If that's you—if somehow you gnawed on spiritual meat before you even tried a bottle of milk—find yourself an Einstein to tutor you. Find someone to school you who understands what spiritual genius is: A simple love for the Music.

CREATIVE EXERCISE: *It's never too late to begin at the beginning. If you feel you skipped a grade in the elementary stages of your spiritual life, now's the time to learn and grow. Take a seminary class, or join a basic Bible study, or pick up a book on the fundamentals of the faith. And if you're stuck creatively on beginning that huge project, or that life-work, try giving it just ten minutes of your time this week.*

5

SCARY SACRIFICES

Art is good when it springs from necessity.
This kind of origin is the guarantee of its value;
there is no other.

—NEAL CASSADY

*P*erhaps you're familiar with the brooding story of
Abraham and Isaac: After God gives Abraham the son of
his dreams, the patriarch is then asked to sacrifice him. Just
as Abraham raises the knife, however, the angel of the Lord intervenes and tells him, "Now I know you fear God, because you have
not withheld from me your son, your only son" (Gen. 22:12 NIV).
God then generously provides a ram for the sacrifice instead.

We know that, just as God has promised him, Abraham goes on to
be the father of many nations. What we're not told in the story is if he
ever spent any time looking over his shoulder, wondering if the whole
sacrifice-ordeal might occur again. Truly, this was a veddddy scary inci-
dent. Abraham almost watched his dreams go up in smoke. Literally.

As artists, we often go through dry spells—seasons of trudging
up the steep mountain of creative sacrifice. At times it seems as if
the very passion of God-glory birthed in our hearts has shriveled up
and disappeared, like a small, burnt offering drifting into the gray
smoke of oblivion. You may smell the scent of art, but there are no
tangible reminders. Only memories. And when the muse or the
music or the dance returns, it's hard not to wonder if it will disappear wispily once again.

"Faith," whispers the writer of Hebrews, "is the substance of things hoped for, the evidence of things not seen" (Heb. 11:1 NKJV). The word "substance" implies *weightiness*. Heavy. Not wispy or shriveled or lightweight. It's hope with some lamb chop on its bones. So you're not singing or writing or drawing or dancing or cooking or entertaining right now? Do you hope to? Do you dare even to . . . pray to? Then don't worry: The Isaac of your art is not dead. It will not die on the makeshift altar of your procrastination, your depression, your fear.

Your faith, your belief in the substance of things hoped for, is the sacrificial ram you offer God—just like the one provided for Abraham in the hour of his darkness. Your main calling isn't necessarily your art. It's to remain tuned in, faithful, obedient in the moment.

Your main calling in this life, like Abraham's, is to have faith.

Maybe it's not worth wasting time looking over your shoulder for either the sword of creative hard times or the unexpected gift of artistic blessing. You often can't control either, anyway. But you *can* see your fear for what it is: Nothing less than guerilla warfare waged against the beauty of the holy lurking within your heart. And you can honestly confront and name your fears, one by one, until they're clearly revealed as the slimy, trench-coat-and-dark-sunglasses wearing boogeymen that they really are.

Here are some favorite fear-mantras of artists: *I'm losing valuable time. It's too late in my life to get started anyway. I will never create again. Everyone is better than I am. I'm not being a good steward. Art is a luxury anyway—who needs it? If I tried harder, things would get better.*

This might sound corny, but try writing those fears on 3 x 5 index cards (even different colored cards for different types of fears—you may see an interesting pattern!). The more the better. You'll need them for the big bonfire you'll have when you invite your friends over for a "fear barbeque." (Pray over the cards, one by one—then throw them into the roasting pit.) Add some burgers and hot dogs, and you've got those gnarly geezers grilled . . . for God's sake.

So, if you're not creating right now, you can still "non-create" out of faith—faith that your artistic longings are still intact, faith in the goodness of God, faith in remaining faithful despite trenchcoat-and-film-noir creative circumstances.

Just like Abraham.

PRAYER: *God, grant me the substance of faith, even when my life—or my creative dream—is shrouded in darkness.*

6

SEEING IN BLACK AND WHITE

Celebrate what you want to see more of.

—THOMAS J. PETERS

*G*erman director Wim Wenders's poignant 1993 film, *Faraway, So Close,* begins with a quote from the book of Matthew and a swooping, aerial view of Berlin—an introduction to the perspective of the two main characters, Damiel and Cassiel. The two share a penchant for tall buildings (most especially winged monuments). And for wearing trendy black overcoats. They are angels.

As the two celestial beings tenderly care for their human wards, walking through city streets, subways, and neighborhoods, we glimpse the world through their compassionate eyes. Damiel and Cassiel ache with unspeakable love for those they watch over. We observe as they sweetly reach out to stroke a face, ruffle hair, whisper soothingly to the sufferings and longings before them. Yet the people in their care cannot see or hear them. As angels, Damiel and Cassiel cannot intervene in matters of human pain or desire; they can only remain an unseen, caring presence.

In the film, the angels' perspective is always shown in black and white—while the human beings in the story are portrayed in color. Yet Wenders' use of black and white film in this regard is not traditional. Usually, black and white offers a flat perspective— reveals something that lacks depth. For Wenders, it's just the opposite: "Black and white reveals the essence of a person, I think, more than a portrait in color," he says. "The angels are spiritual beings. They'd see the truth much more than we can—and for me, colors are very much the surface of things."

As a filmmaker, Wenders is *definitely* concerned with much more than the surface of things. *Faraway, So Close* portrays angels literally—not as metaphorical figures or symbols, but as heavenly beings who brood like doves over this world, much like poet Gerard Manley Hopkins's image of the Spirit in "God's Grandeur," *with warm breast and with ah! bright wings.* They are silent nurturers, quiet comforters. Reminders of God's ever-present care.

The movie traces Damiel and Cassiel's decisions to become human—the two do so for entirely different reasons—until the film's tragic but redemptive ending. Their last words haunt us as we leave their comforting presence to continue our earthbound, color-filled existence: *You, whom we love. You do not see us, you do not hear us, you imagine us in the far distance, yet we are so near . . . . We are not the message, we are the messengers. The message is love . . . . Let us dwell in your eyes, see your world through us. Recapture through us that loving look once again. Then we will be close to you—and you to him.*

Their gentle words bring to mind the Scripture passage that opens the film, Matthew 6:22: "The eye is the lamp of the body. If your eyes are good, your whole body will be full of light" (NIV). See as we do, the angels say. See through the eyes of love.

The spare luxury of love in art needs no adornment, as Wim Wenders' use of black and white demonstrates in *Faraway, So Close.* Stark, simple—but true, sincere. Beautiful. That's why, in an artistic culture that values creative excellence above all things, a simple truth can set us free: *A work of art created through the eyes of love is always a masterpiece.*

That which is birthed and delivered in love is beloved of God.

Perhaps Paul's words in Philippians 1 are the artist's creed, both for life and created things:

"So this is my prayer: that your love will flourish and that you will not only love much but well. Learn to love appropriately. You need to use your head and test your feelings so that your love is sincere and intelligent, not sentimental gush. Live a lover's life, circumspect and exemplary, a life Jesus will be proud of: bountiful in fruits from the soul, making Jesus Christ attractive to all, getting everyone involved in the glory and praise of God" (vv. 9–11 *The Message*).

May you color your world with such love, as you explore the power of seeing in black and white.

CREATIVE MEDITATION: *Nothing is sweeter than love, nothing stronger, nothing higher, nothing wider, nothing more pleasant, nothing fuller or better in heaven or in earth; for love is born of God, and cannot rest but in God, above all created things.*

—THOMAS À KEMPIS, *The Imitation of Christ*

7

TRUTH-TELLING AND NAKEDNESS

Tell truth, and shame the devil.

—JONATHAN SWIFT

ruth-telling is both humbling and frightening. Kind of like those scary adolescent dreams in which you stand stark naked in front of your high school biology class, with no place to hide. Zits and all.

Judging from everything we read in the Bible, God is the consummate truth-teller. You have to hand it to him: He's definitely not into image management. If he were, he most assuredly would've sanitized the sordid account of King David's life. Or banned the embarrassing story of Noah and his sons (the part where nudity and drunkenness were involved). Or at least tidied up the story of Jacob so he wouldn't seem like the greasy weasel he was—more like a slick used-car salesman than a shining saint.

Biblical writing is honest, no-holds-barred writing. And because of that, we have an incredibly challenging artistic precedent to follow. Good art is truth-telling. It's precisely because God *didn't* clean up the stories of the lives of his people that we catch glimpses of both who he is and who we are. And aren't. The God who spoke loudly through a braying donkey is the same God who longs to create gold-glints of glory and grace from the gray ash pits of our lives. The same God who spoke through the once-cowardly, two-faced Peter desires to lay hands on our own scaredy-cat voices and use them to bugle-call blessing and hope to those around us.

The poet T. S. Eliot once made a telling comment about religious writing. He said that most of it fails because the writers don't write about how they really feel—they write about how they *want* to feel. So true. Many of us shrink from writing or creating truthfully about faith because of a dogged commitment to image management. Image management is all about looking good. It's so you can look mahvelous, dahling. And when you give into the lure of image management, you end up telling your story or creating characters who always choose rightly in moments of temptation, who only say what's wise and noble in stressful situations—who don't battle with lust and greed and self-deceptive spirituality.

Unlike the great Bible characters we admire. (Thank goodness, they didn't have agents.)

It's pretty hard to be a truth-teller and hold onto any sort of spiritual hubris. That's because resisting the urge to sanitize what we write—whether it is our own story or one of our own creation—is so humbling, and so like God. It's a tough task. When our spirituality acts as a self-protective cloak over our souls or over our art, it's a good time to get back to the basic Bible—an epic story where warts can be redeemed:

"God wants us to grow up, to know the whole truth and tell it in love—like Christ in everything," says Paul. "What this adds up to, then, is this: no more lies, no more pretense. Tell your neighbor the truth. In Christ's body we're all connected to each other, after all" (Eph. 4:15, 25 *The Message*).

To be an artistic truth-teller of faith is a bit like reliving that troubling adolescent dream, with one major difference: We can afford to be exposed when we know we're fully clothed in grace and mercy. To be a truth-teller means we don't have to flee in horror and shame from our heart's nakedness, knowing our shivering souls are blanketed by the warm, unpatronizing love of One who is truth— One who sees all clearly, and yet covers us completely.

Just as Noah's sons once did for him.

CREATIVE EXERCISE: *Truth is the word of the week. Let it take you somewhere . . . creative.*

8

PLAYING BY
BILL ROMANOWSKI'S RULES

> *Do you not know that those who run in*
> *a race all run, but only one receives the prize?*
> *Run in such a way that you may win.*
> —1 CORINTHIANS 9:24 NASB

S ome athletes talk about the loose-and-limber connections they're able to make between their physical exercise and their spiritual lives: Work out hard. Be disciplined. Stay focused. Often, in order to fine-tune their athletic skills, they engage in activities that might seem absurd: Basketball players hop on one foot up the bleachers to develop their rebounding abilities. Two-hundred-and-sixty-pound linebackers feverishly tiptoe across the football field in order to gain greater balance and coordination.

Here in Denver, Bronco linebacker Bill Romanowski takes a lot of teasing from his teammates for his bizarre, frog-legged warm-up routines. But they work. "Romo," as he is affectionately known here in the Mile-High City, is a fierce competitor on the field—helping lead the Broncos to two world championships. But that's partly because he has a double life: He cross-trains . . . as a ballerina. And it makes Romo one awesome football player.

If you want to embrace a creative calling, it's important to dispel a pervasive myth: That you should only focus on creative activities. One of the biggest misconceptions about artists is that fulfillment and creative growth are found only in "creating" all the time.

You know—right-brain stuff. No analytical exegesis of biblical passages. No systematic study of psychological theories. No investigation into the origins of crankshaft and carburetor problems. In other words, the myth is that "those creative types" should stick solely to those more flaky, fringe activities in order to fulfill their calling as artists.

Yet right- and left-brain cross-training is vital to the work of art. For instance, our sense of rhythm in music and poetry comes from the left side of the brain, not the right. That's what orders the beats, counts the measures. In order to achieve a sense of artful balance, it's important to recognize that neither side of the brain is more important than the other. Reading fiction can make us more fervent, less-frivolous theologians. Writing poetry can help us be more passionate, penetrating psychologists. Creating colorful collages can invite us to be more curious, careful car mechanics.

Another myth is that if we're good at something like pencil sketching or interior decorating or flower arranging, we shouldn't spread ourselves too thin and lose our artistic concentration by attempting sculpture or filmmaking or clothes design. Yet creativity—like athletic training—works precisely contrary to a purely surface view of things. Creativity is like a vast pool where every tributary, every sparkling brook, both branches off the pool and waters it as well. By taking risks, opening ourselves up to new artistic avenues, we stretch the muscles of our souls; we limber up the unused joints of our minds; we plié in order to be better artistic players on the fields of our dreams.

To run the race to win as an artist is to risk looking foolish by exercising everything we have, body and soul, for the sake of winning the prize of Christ's presence in our art. For the sake of winning *him*. To others, that may look as strange as Bill Romanowski's weird warm-up routine. In fact, it's bound to. Here's how one twentieth-century thinker describes this dilemma:

"Society demands [that] . . . each must stand at his post, here a cobbler, there a poet. No man is expected to be both. Such a man would be 'different' from other people, not quite reliable. . . . In short, he would always be suspected of unreliability and incompetence, because society is persuaded that only the cobbler who is not a poet can supply workmanlike shoes."

This is what society thinks . . . but not God. That theologian Jesus was also a poet. And a storyteller. And a prophet. And a psychologist. And probably a car mechanic, if he'd lived in our time. (He *was*, after all, a carpenter to boot.)

So break free of cultural expectations in order to train your heart, soul, and mind with all your strength. Are you interested in block printmaking? Try it. Want to study Egyptian hieroglyphics? Do it. Itching to try your hand at acting? Go for it. And at the same time, include some ballet exercises—and read St. Ignatius of Loyola or John Calvin. Or Carl Jung.

That's playing by Bill Romanowski's rules.

CREATIVE EXERCISE: *This is your week to dabble. What's that intriguing art form you know nothing about? Try jumping in—no, diving in head first—and see what happens. Pick up a book on interior design, visit a pottery studio, sign up for singing lessons. As the sports commercial says, "Just do it."*

9

PARTY ANIMALS FOR CHRIST

*Essential characteristics of the really great
novelists: a Christlike, all-embracing compassion.*

—ARNOLD BENNETT

hat is forgiveness, really? And why forgive? What
does it have to do with art?

Jesus was a relentless forgiver—and taught a relentless
forgiveness. In Matthew 18, when Peter wagers a guess as to how
many times he should forgive, he rolls the dice and comes up with
what he thinks is a winning number: seven. (From what we know
of Peter, he probably thought this would really impress Jesus—once
again pushing the edge of the faithful-follower-envelope.) Jesus
replies, "Seven! Hardly. Try seventy times seven." Christ then tells a
vivid tale about a mean-spirited servant. The king of the region for-
gives this servant a hundred-thousand-dollar debt—and the servant responds to this act of mercy by immediately demanding that
one of his friends pay up on a measly ten-dollar debt. Unbelievable!
Christ is saying: That's what each of you is like when you don't forgive unconditionally anyone who asks to be forgiven (see Matt.
18:21–35 in *The Message*).

Yet forgiveness is a difficult art of the soul. And sometimes a fresh
artistic perspective on the process—what it looks like both to give
and need forgiveness, or even to feel forgiven—can move and change
us the most. Art can transform a dry theological topic into one much
more desperate, much more human. And much more needed.

Some novels in recent years have tackled the subject from a variety of perspectives. Take, for example, Anne Tyler's *Saint Maybe*. The main character, Ian Bedloe, is a young man consumed with guilt over his role in several tragic family circumstances. His quest for peace leads him to join the congregation of the Church of the Second Chance, which is exactly what it purports to be. *Why is it so difficult to feel forgiven?* the novel asks. Ian fleshes out our struggle, including the drastic measures we often take to do penance.

In Oscar Hijuelos's *Mr. Ives' Christmas* a father agonizes over his son's senseless murder. His faith in God is shaken. Why forgive? And how? The novel gently leads us by the hand through one man's daily experience—an experience of both grief and hope. We become part of the story by connecting with the main character through our own ambivalent feelings about tragic and seemingly unjust losses.

Ron Hansen's *Atticus* is also a remarkable portrayal of forgiveness. The book's premise centers firmly around a very familiar biblical passage, but we get so absorbed in the narrative that only at the end do we realize we've simply read the Bible in new and novel fashion. Oh, we say—so that's what forgiveness looks like.

Jesus' lengthiest teaching on forgiveness is, of course, a story. It revolves around a renegade son—one who squanders the family inheritance and causes his father's name great shame. When the son finally returns home, he expects to be hired on as a lowly field-worker, and certainly not to be received again as a son. But that isn't what happens, as you know. Instead, his father comes flying pell-mell down the road right toward him, arms open, crying his eyes out. He's overjoyed to have his boy back. And not only that, but he's ordered the T-bones put on the grill for the biggest party imaginable (see Luke 15:11–32).

If Jesus throws big parties for his prodigal sons and daughters who return, then why not throw big forgiveness-parties for one another?

To forgive really passionately, however, we need to become party animals: We've got to receive a big forgiveness-bash before we can host one for someone else. That's because Jesus says whoever is forgiven little, loves little—but that those who are forgiven much love much (see Luke 7:47).

Since throwing good parties requires creative preparation, how about preparing our souls for forgiveness in the same way? Go ahead: run through your grocery list of oughts. Think of those little munchies, name them one by one. Count your many blessings, see what God has done. The roast beef of the matter is that we've probably been forgiven of things just as bad—and probably worse. The longer our shopping list of things we've received forgiveness for, the better our celebrations will be for others.

A Jewish thinker said that one characteristic of true repentance is increased creativity. He believed a clear sign that someone had received God's forgiveness was the creation of good art.

If that's true, then the novelists Anne Tyler, Oscar Hijuelos, and Ron Hansen might just know what it's like to be forgiven. As their novels portray so eloquently, forgiveness isn't just a rote concept—it's a loving story to be entered into, moved by, touched, felt. And, according to Jesus' story, each time we ask for forgiveness or we forgive, it's cause for wild celebration. Party on, dude.

CREATIVE SPIRITUAL EXERCISE: *What do you need to know you're forgiven of in order to freely throw kingdom parties for others? Or maybe you've never known what it's like to celebrate at Christ's party of grace. Now's your time. Try creating something this week that reflects the wonder of gratitude.*

10

THERE GOES ART . . .
ACTING UP AGAIN

All the poet can do is warn.
That is why true poets must be truthful.

—WILFRED OWEN

*G*wendolyn Brooks, the first African-American woman poet to win the Pulitzer Prize, once described her goal for writing. In 1967, Brooks says, she made a conscious shift in her literary direction. From that time forward, she chose to focus her work almost exclusively on the continuing problem of racism in America. She said, "What I'm fighting for now in my work [is] an expression relevant to all manner of blacks, poems I could take into a tavern, into the street, into the halls of a housing project." In short, she had a clear-eyed commitment to portray the harsh realities of urban African-American life. And one of the best examples of this is found in her short poem, "We Real Cool." Her compact, sparse word-picture of young, pool-playing black men is one of the most anthologized poems of all time.

The poet Denise Levertov observed that poetry always has a social effect, regardless of whether the poet intends it to. Poetry as social power may seem a quaint thought, especially in a pragmatic culture that ascribes political power to the daily grind of the sound-bite machinery. One-dimensional, prosaic slogans such as, "Let's return to family values" often dominate the expression of Christ that's written across our culture. Yet the glory of poetry—and all forms of art—is that it can transcend all manner of such mundane barriers. *Artists of the soul are* creative *social activists.* They dare to venture into hidden heart-corners—neglected regions of the soul where strident slogans are suddenly turned into touching, human heartbreaks or joys.

In 1945, Gwendolyn Brooks wrote the following poem. She took a subject that was particularly taboo for its time, but that today is regularly held up as a political cause. And, somehow, she mysteriously transformed it into the holy bond of shared pathos and suffering:

THE MOTHER

Abortions will not let you forget.
You remember the children you got that you did not get,
The damp small pulps with a little or with no hair,
The singers and workers that never handled the air.
You will never neglect or beat
Them, or silence or buy with a sweet.
You will never wind up the sucking-thumb
Or scuttle off ghosts that come.
You will never leave them, controlling your luscious sigh,
Return for a snack of them, with gobbling mother-eye.

I have heard in the voices of the wind the voices of my dim
    killed children.
I have contracted. I have eased
My dim dears at the breasts they could never suck.
I have said, Sweets, if I sinned, if I seized
Your luck
And your lives from your unfinished reach,

If I stole your births and your names,
Your straight baby tears and your games,
Your stilted or lovely loves, your tumults, your marriages,
    aches, and your deaths,
If I poisoned the beginnings of your breaths,
Believe that even in my deliberateness I was not deliberate.
Though why should I whine,
Whine that the crime was other than mine?—
Since anyhow you are dead.
Or rather, or instead,
You were never made.

But that too, I am afraid,
Is faulty: oh, what shall I say, how is the truth to be said?
You were born, you had body, you died.
It is just that you never giggled or planned or cried.

Believe me, I loved you all.
Believe me, I knew you, though faintly, and I loved, I loved
    you,
All.

The poet's portrayal of a mother's ache over her dead children
burrows into our own hearts—and festers as a soul-wound. The
poem disturbs us, makes us think. We cannot help but be deeply
affected by its sense of longing and regret.

Kathleen Raine says the poet affects our society because "he/she
is the explorer, the opener of the way, one who ventures, in a state
of inspiration, into regions of consciousness which in most of us

remain dark and unexplored." And as Gwendolyn Brooks's moving poem demonstrates so beautifully, the artist as social activist creates works that accurately portray the human condition—works that tell the truth, that let the political blue-chips fall where they may.

Artists of the soul can venture in a state of inspiration—the inspiration of the Holy Spirit—into cultural territory that remains dark and unexplored. Through dependence on those telltale tail-lights ahead of you, you can dare to be an artist who is unafraid not only to take "the road less traveled," but to opt for the road never *before* traveled.

PRAYER: *Merciful God, may what my heart and hands create cross cultural barriers, scale walls, build bridges. May what I create portray not just a value, but Love incarnate.*

11

WE'RE ALL A
BUNCH OF MARTHAS

> *A work of art that contains*
> *theories is like an object on which*
> *the price tag has been left.*
> —MARCEL PROUST

*I*magine walking into the foyer of an opulent high-rise and, for a moment, soaking in its luxurious design. You see huge linen curtain swags, embroidered with rich colors of cobalt, violet, and flaming red. Upon closer inspection, you see that the curtains' intricate embroidered design-work resembles a Renaissance painting of cherubim.

You are surrounded by gorgeous, heavy wood paneling. Shining gold lamps are embossed with the intricate buds and blossoms of flowers. A wonderful fragrance permeates the room—what is it? Jasmine? Clove? You can't quite tell. All you know is that your senses are thoroughly sated. For a moment, you pretend this building is where you live, where you work.

Trump Tower in New York City? Hardly. This is a partial description of a building that trumps all of the Donald's holdings: the tabernacle built by Moses and friends in the book of Exodus. And this is one place in the Bible where God calls upon artists to fulfill his heart's desire, to see that his purposes are thoroughly carried out:

"Then Moses said to the Israelites, 'See, the Lord has chosen Bezalel son of Uri, the son of Hur, of the tribe of Judah, and he has filled him with the Spirit of God, with skill, ability and knowledge in all kinds of crafts—to make artistic designs for work in gold, silver and bronze, to cut and set stones, to work in wood and to engage in all kinds of craftsmanship. And he has given both him and Oholiab son of Ahisamach, of the tribe of Dan, the ability to teach others. He has filled them with skill to do all kinds of work as craftsmen, designers, embroiderers in blue, purple and scarlet yarn and fine linen, and weavers—all of them master craftsmen and designers. So Bezalel, Oholiab and every skilled person to whom the Lord has given skill and ability to know how to carry out all the work of constructing the sanctuary are to do the work just as the Lord has commanded'" (Exod. 35:30–36:1 NIV).

These artisans evidently were known among the people for their particular creative abilities and skills. Architecture, interior design, jewelry making, woodworking, metal sculpture, pottery, clothing design—all are highlighted in Exodus 35–40. And the artists' faithful creations are central to God's people's worship of him.

The tabernacle described in Exodus is actually reminiscent of some of the more refreshing trends of postmodern architecture: people-oriented design as opposed to cold modernity, revival of various historical styles, artistic or playful or even humorous touches. The deep, warm colors, the historical cherubim, the elegant gold lamps—this tabernacle's design would fit nicely into our modern culture's landscape of buildings. Yet, unlike so many of our created structures, the tabernacle is designed for the glory of God alone.

Some people claim they're not artists—yet they enjoy the look of their flowered throw pillows arranged on the sofa, just so. Or they like observing the way houses are designed and built—the square or oval shapes of windows, the straight lines of blueprints.

The above passage in Scripture seems to encourage just this kind of artistry. It's a direct affirmation of those who might be drawn to areas such as interior design or architecture, or simply the art of creating a warm, comforting home environment.

The spaces that we live and work in speak so much about our souls—and about our God. Think of it—the tabernacle itself is a splendid foreshadow of Christ: God would spare no expense, even the death of his own Son, in order to purchase his people's hearts. He would bring his finest to the process. And we are invited to do the same in our worship—to bring all our heart, soul, mind, and strength to everything we do.

Including arranging sofa cushions and designing backyard decks.

Today, our bodies serve as the tabernacle of God, the temple of the Holy Spirit. And we ourselves can be that place that resonates with God's love for rich color, his fine eye for detail, his partiality to the aroma of life. Wherever we are, we can create fragrant, sacred space around us—living invitations to worship an incredible Artisan. We can reflect the lavish truth about the One who, long ago, carefully designed the elaborate and intricate detail of his house of worship. Our God simply relishes the fine art of decorating . . . our souls.

In short, we're all really just a bunch of Marthas.

Martha Stewart, that is.

CREATIVE EXERCISE: *Use some creativity this week to add a fresh touch to your home or office. Try something new: colorful flowers, fruit, photos. Or, journal on this idea of creating sacred spaces that reflect your soul—and your God.*

12

SCARRED FOR LIFE

Everyone has talent.
What is rare is the courage to follow the talent
to the dark place where it leads.

—ERICA JONG

*T*he painting is a front-on view into a children's playroom. A colorful rainbow mural hangs on the wall, a friendly sun peeking out from behind its multi-hued arch. Fluffy, woolly clouds graze the mural's top corners. Rows of toys and plastic containers holding art supplies are stacked on shelves. A blue plastic mat is stretched across the floor.

Yet the children we see in the painting are an aching contrast to the cheery scene. A little girl in a yellow and red full body cast leans against the mural, desperately clutching the wall for support, or maybe comfort. The look in her eyes is blank, haunting. There are other children who lie listlessly within this fluorescent-lighted room—in a wheelchair, on the floor under a play mobile, in a bean bag chair. Adult caregivers lean over them, touching them, tenderly shifting their bodies. The clock on the wall tells us it is fifteen minutes until two—the middle of a long, perhaps painful day for these disabled children and those who love them.

The painting is called *Big Picture*.

The artist Tim Lowly's intimate portrayals of disabled children offer us a glimpse into the reality of this bigger picture, this larger world outside our own. The artist first began creating his touching works by painting his own daughter, Temma, who has limited mobility and is unable to see or speak. Lowly's work is characterized by its vulnerability—a quiet, attentive view of suffering that is refreshingly free of sentimental pity. His compassionate, realistic paintings remind us again of heartache that hovers just outside the door of our own daily lives, in nicely tucked-away hospital rooms or non-descript hospices or private bedrooms.

This same vulnerable realism, this tenacious lack of sentimentality, is also seen in the work of the Texas poet Vassar Miller, who recently passed away. Miller, a lifelong sufferer from cerebral palsy, wrote ten books of poetry, one of them a finalist for the Pulitzer Prize in 1961. Her poems are both heartbreaking and hope-filled. The poet professed a deep and living faith in God, even while struggling fiercely with the bitter pain of her own imprisoned body. Her searingly honest work chronicles a life of desperate emotional and physical loss.

A *Houston Chronicle* reviewer wrote of Miller's poems, "Her subjects are the same ones that keep most people searching beyond and beneath the surfaces of their daily lives: love, life, emotions and the unfilled longings of the disabled." In this article about Miller's poetry, the writer fingers the nerve of truth that runs underneath the delicate skins of each of our own souls: No matter who we are, no matter where we live, we each carry within us the unfilled longings of the disabled. We are each crippled, broken, shattered. We each bear sorrow's shared scars of the heart.

And, as artists of the soul, we also can help turn one another's scars into art.

Our soul-scarred art is a means for expression, comfort, meaning. Yet it's also a process that encourages physical healing. In fact, medical studies have documented art's healing power: People suffering from asthma and arthritis show dramatic improvements in symptoms when they write about traumatic experiences in their lives. It has also been proven that rhythm, harmony, and melody activate the cerebellum—the region of the brain that controls coordination and balance. Art is a salve—not only for our souls, but for our physical bodies as well.

Through the power of faith, the art that emerges from our deepest sorrows also serves as a bridge between us. It is art that can transform our losses and griefs into the mysteries of holy comfort: "Blessed be the God and Father of our Lord Jesus Christ," Paul writes, "the Father of all mercies and God of all comfort, who comforts us in all our suffering, so that we may be able to comfort those who are suffering with the comfort we have received from God" (2 Cor. 1:3–4). The art that emerges from our own brokenness is part of God's own passion to take care of his broken people.

The God of all comfort lives in the work of artists such as Tim Lowly or Vassar Miller—artists who create from the truth of this world's suffering. And soul-artists who create sorrow's art not only can bring healing to others, but often experience the wonder of God's comfort for themselves.

The scars of the heart are a part of the bigger picture of Art.

CREATIVE SPIRITUAL EXERCISE: *What can you create this week that reflects the truth about someone else's suffering? About your own?*

13

GOODNESS, GRACIOUS, GREAT GOBS OF GOOD NEWS

> *Religion and art spring from*
> *the same root and are close kin.*
>
> —WILLA CATHER

Leonardo da Vinci's *The Annunciation* (circa 1472) is a gorgeous rendition of God's often surprising life-interruptions. In the painting, the angel Gabriel kneels before Mary, announcing the startling news that she is to be the mother of the much-awaited Messiah. As she listens to this stunning good news, Mary raises her left hand in greeting. Yet her right arm remains casually draped across the plain linen of her sewing project. Her pose is a portrait of the cathedral of common life.

In this study in contrasts, da Vinci captures the essence of how the greatest news in history arrived. His portrayal is reminiscent of how the Prince of all Princes appeared as he was crowned from his mother's womb—and ushered into the castle of a funky, rickety, wooden stable. Very ordinary.

The "good news of great joy to all people" often arrives to us as it did to Mary: in ordinary ways, outside the church's walls. The Messiah speaks through the "Hallelujah Chorus," yes—but he also wants us to get a handle on his use of more ordinary means. God doesn't want us to miss the more common, soul-shattering moments when, like da Vinci's painting, our soul's history is transformed by his surprising interruptions—in the time that elapses between two stitches in a piece of muslin. He still sends his angel, today, to us—in the form of the Holy Spirit. As the angel came to Mary long ago, so the Holy Spirit comes to us, to continually remind us of the eternal good news of great joy, that has come to all the people. The Spirit's job is to remind us of the words of Christ.

That angel of good news, God's Spirit, can arrive like a careful grocery clerk while we're poking through the disappointment of green strawberries in the produce section of the grocery store. Suddenly, we remember that he's the vine, we're the branches . . . and apart from him we can do nothing, nothing, nothing. Oh boy, do we know *that.*

But hope bursts like a berry when we encounter a gorgeous, red, ripe piece of fruit. When he prunes us it's so we can be lip-smackingly fruitful, dripping with the fresh juice of his Spirit. *Keep up the work, O Gardener of souls,* we say, as we dig through the good, the bad, and the ugly, remembering that he continues to dig, too. *You say you see a seed in us worth cultivating and harvesting, and that you will be faithful to complete your work in us.*

The angel of good news arrives like a tissue-carrying friend as we sniffle joyously when Meg Ryan and Tom Hanks finally meet at the top of the Empire State Building in *Sleepless in Seattle. Yeah, this is great,* the remembered verse whispers, *and just think: You haven't even seen or imagined or even allowed it to enter your heart the things God's got prepared someday for all of you who are in love with* him.

The angel of good news can arrive like a dutiful garbage collector when we're tying up the smelly plastic bags in the kitchen, bags dripping with fetid coffee grounds, half-eaten hamburgers, paper towels dripping with bacon grease. *Why don't you get rid of all this garbage,* the Word reminds us, *all this malice and guile and hypocrisy and slander? Just tie it up in a big bag and throw it out. Otherwise, you'll stink up and ruin the warm, mealtime places in your soul.*

The words of redemption are like great gobs of goodness, sticking like bubble gum to our souls. They stick to everything we think, do, say, feel, dislike, hope for, want, *imagine.* "Imagine" is the key word here: Leonardo da Vinci used his imagination to artistically create a biblical scene that erupts with the rich, warm fabric of ordinary life. In the same way, the Holy Spirit is the artistic director in the workshop of the soul—the source of inspiration and imagination in our everyday lives. Like da Vinci did in his portrayal of Mary, the imaginative Spirit paints the word of God to life while we sort produce, watch movies, haul out the trash.

The Holy Spirit's creative job is to continually make real to us Christ's words—and to help us remember everything he said—in all we do: "The Friend, the Holy Spirit whom the Father will send at my request, will make everything plain to you," Jesus said. "He will remind you of all the things I have told you" (John 14:26 *The Message*).

Like the angel of the Lord with Mary in da Vinci's painting, the Holy Spirit wants to visit us, talk to us, prepare our hearts for a Messiah who will one day come again—and, that time, in definite Hallelujah Chorus fashion. Until then, he performs a most imaginative job while we, like Mary, live our most common lives: He helps the great gobs of good news stick fast to our souls like ordinary, pink bubble gum.

SCRIPTURE MEDITATION: *(Jesus is speaking to his disciples.) "But when the Friend comes, the Spirit of the Truth, he will take you by the hand and guide you into all the truth there is"* (John 16:13 *The Message*).

14

WEARING OUR WEAPONS WELL

Art is mighty; for art is the work
of man under the guidance and inspiration
of a mightier power than man.

—J. C. HARE

*T*here's a certain section of Scripture that reads like a fashion-catalog description for a fairy-tale character. When Paul lists the spiritual weapons necessary for battle-ready faith, the passage conjures vivid images of brawny knights arming themselves for battle: "Stand firm then, with the belt of truth buckled around your waist, with the breastplate of righteousness in place, and with your feet fitted with the readiness that comes from the gospel of peace," he says. "In addition to all this, take up the shield of faith, with which you can extinguish all the flaming arrows of the evil one. Take the helmet of salvation and the sword of the Spirit, which is the word of God" (Eph. 6:14–17 NIV).

Perhaps filmmaker Pierre Sauvage had this passage in mind when he titled his 1989 documentary *Weapons of the Spirit.* Yet the film is definitely no fairy tale: It is the amazing story of how the tiny Christian community of Le Chambon-sur-Lignon, France, successfully sheltered over 5,000 Jews during World War II—*while the village was occupied by Nazis.*

Sauvage himself was born in Le Chambon and hidden during a time when several members of his family were dying in concentration camps. When he was four, he and his parents moved to New

York City. After becoming a filmmaker, Sauvage started the Chambon Foundation in 1982, a nonprofit educational foundation that explores experiences—and lessons—of hope that took place during the Holocaust.

Some forty years after the war, Sauvage returned to Le Chambon with his film crew to document the story of the Christians who willingly faced death to protect their Jewish brothers and sisters. Over and over in the film, the citizens of Le Chambon recount incidents for which divine intervention is the only explanation of how they were able to maintain their vast "conspiracy of goodness." For instance, they tell of Nazi soldiers who routinely forgot to look around just one corner, or failed to see obviously Jewish people standing right in front of their faces, just inches away. Yet the villagers seem almost casual when describing the details of their own heroic measures. "We did what we had to do," an old woman shrugs. "What can I say?" These people simply—and unwaveringly—believed it was their spiritual responsibility to risk their lives. Anything less would have been unthinkable.

The villagers of Le Chambon beautifully portray both the shining satin—and the casual cotton—of the weapons of our warfare, which are the weapons of the Spirit. On one hand, if we do not believe in the reality of evil—the reality that there is reason to battle and wage war in the heavenlies, in spiritual realms—then we have dressed neither appropriately nor elegantly for the occasion of Christianity. These French Christians relied fervently on the meek power of prayer—and their act of faith brought a spiritual sword down on the sleek, diabolical neck of Hitler's reign of terror.

On the other hand, dressing for spiritual battle should be made out of the natural fibers of our being. More like the comfortable fit of old jeans than a sequined tuxedo that blares through noisy books and radio programs, "Watch out for demons! Beware the enemy! Pray down those strongholds!" When you truly *do* believe that evil exists, as these villagers did, then you are more likely to take at face value that good—and God—are always stronger, and that you have a part in that battle. Then, when you pray and arm yourself with truth and peace and every other piece of battle equipment Paul describes, you'll do so with the appropriate shrug of "I'm only doing what I'm *supposed* to be doing." Anything less, as the villagers of Le Chambon believed, would be unthinkable.

The world we live in is no fairy tale—and artists especially are waging a dark, oppressive war. That's why it's time to get serious about the daily spiritual battle we face. Through the example of our brothers and sisters from Le Chambon, we can learn much about the mysterious-yet-common weapons of the Spirit.

It only takes a village, you know.

PRAYER: *Lord, it's humbling to contemplate my brothers and sisters in the faith who once risked their lives in the midst of war. Allow my art to be one of your weapons of the Spirit in the world.*

15

OF CALLING AND ICE CAPADES

On with dance,
let joy be unconfined, is my motto.

—MARK TWAIN

writer friend tells this story: One icy Manhattan after-
noon, he was walking and talking with a prima ballerina for
the New York City Ballet. Just ahead of him my friend saw
a twenty-five- to thirty-foot stretch of black ice. Just for fun, he ran
about three steps and took a glide, turning to face the dancer as he slid
backward on the ice, continuing to chat.

The ballerina didn't follow him. Rather, she walked gingerly
around the ice while my friend waited for her to catch up. As they
continued their stroll, she said to my friend, "Oh, I wish I could do
what you just did." My friend said, "Well, why don't you? The ice
is right back there—go ahead, I'll wait for you."

She shook her head no. My friend was puzzled. "Why on earth
can't you?" he asked. "Because I'm a dancer," she said, "and we're
too clumsy to do things like that." At first that seemed absurd to
him—his ballerina friend was one of the most physically graceful
people he'd ever known. But then it struck him: Because of her level
of sheer grace, experiencing the slightest bit of awkwardness made
her feel clumsy. She was so disciplined in dance grace that anything
less felt too ungraceful, on stage or off.

Her words reminded him of a Picasso pen-and-ink sketch he'd
seen not long before at the Museum of Modern Art, a drawing of

three female dancers *en pointe*. The sketch captured uncannily the perfection of the three dancers' line. But they looked grotesque, because Picasso drew all three women as grossly overweight.

The drawing so vividly captured what his ballerina friend felt, and what many dancers often feel about themselves, regardless of how graceful and physically fit they are; they think of themselves as clumsy, fat, and inept. And, metaphorically speaking, so do a lot of artists, regardless of their trade. When you've once tasted the bliss of effortlessness, it's as if you're a failure when you savor anything less.

Sometimes, those who are most abundantly drenched in creative graces or gifts are the ones who are most deeply aware of their every shortfall, their every departure from the high standard. Let's face it: Artists are notorious perfectionists. And if we're honest, we all have times when not only our art but our *souls* feel hopelessly klutzy—as if we'd put on our biblical ballerina shoes backward. When you desire angelic arabesques, it's downright demoralizing to dance as if the devil were chasing you: awkward, off-beat, your soul splayed crazily like a bad plié.

Yet those are great artistic moments—the gentle reminder that our calling is something much more than mere spiritual discipline can ever spark. Our high calling goes far beyond human effort; it is generated by the Spirit's leaping tongues of fire: "You are a chosen people," says Peter, "a royal priesthood, a holy nation, a people belonging to God, that you may declare the praises of him who called you out of darkness into his wonderful light" (1 Pet. 2:9 NIV).

Our pulled hamstrings leave us with a limp that reminds us we're dependent on the Spirit to dance his way across the stage of our souls. The Spirit gently wrestles us again and again to the ground, saying, "How can you know the Dancer from the dance?

By knowing the dance is not center stage—the Dancer is. By knowing that the point isn't your mistakes or your successes, but the praises of him who called you out of darkness into the brilliant spotlight of the glory of God."

That's when we can get up off our knees, energized, renewed, allowing our shortcomings to propel us more passionately into the dance of life. We can dare to slide crazily on the icy spiritual terrain in front of us, knowing that being clumsy and awkward is the caper of Christ's calling. It takes more humility to leap onto the dance floor in faith, stepping on toes and tripping over our own feet, than to be a spiritual wallflower, hugging the boring folding chairs of our pride for safety.

Our tastes of sublimity are enjoyable, sure. But for the other ninety-nine percent of life when we're struggling with the most basic steps in our biblical ballet, sheer, adoring passion for the glory of the Dancer will do.

That's what you call "grace-full" dancing.

PRAYER: *Please lead me in the dance of redemption, God. Help me to take risks in this world for your sake. Even this week, show me what it means for me to get out of my folding chair and to dance for your pleasure.*

16

I Love to Tell the Story . . .

I would rather be remembered
by a song than by a victory.
—ALEXANDER SMITH

*M*argaret Guenther, author of *Holy Listening: The Art of Spiritual Direction,* speaks of the director's role as that of a spiritual midwife. Those who tenderly assist in matters of the heart are like careful midwives, she says, attending to what Meister Eckhart calls "the birth of God in the soul." Spiritual directors hold the heart-hands of those they care for—encouraging them through the various transitional stages of Christ's likeness being formed within them and birthed without.

Artists often act as "spiritual midwives" to one another during the birthing process of a new creation. Every creator is acquainted with the flutters of excitement over possibility, the ache and uncomfortability of the gestation period, the hard work and very particular pain of labor, and the sheer joy of giving birth to a new, sometimes squalling, work of art. So what better person to attend to the needs of an artist but another artist? A bond exists between those who know what occurs in the hushed or chaotic rooms where a work of art is born. There's an unspoken respect for the process, a sympathetic understanding of the cost.

As artists of the soul, we have a unique privilege: to care for one another's works of art as if they were our very own. We can embrace the honor of bringing flowers, wiping tired brows, saying soothing prayers for those who labor in our circle of creative friends. We can remember to record the memorable moments in one another's lives, to take "snapshots of the soul"—and to pull out our scrapbook of memories when others most need to be reminded of pictures of God's grace in the past. Sometimes, we might even be asked to serve as godparents to one another's works—to take responsibility, before God, to help nurture and care and provide for the artistic offspring of those we love.

"If you've gotten anything at all out of following Christ," Paul says, "if his love has made any difference in your life, if being in a community of the Spirit means anything to you, if you have a heart, if you *care*—then do me a favor: Agree with each other, love each other, be deep-spirited friends. Don't push your way to the front; don't sweet-talk your way to the top. Put yourself aside, and help others get ahead. Don't be obsessed with getting your own advantage. Forget yourselves long enough to lend a helping hand" (Phil. 2:1–4 *The Message*).

This is what distinguishes the art of the artist of the soul. We're not only called to become the best artist we can possibly be; we're also called to make others *better than ourselves*. To have our influence bear visible fruit in the lives—and art—of people whose creative work we've delighted in, constructively criticized, encouraged, financed, sought to provide artistic opportunities for—*until they've surpassed us, and long after.*

There's much more to our lives as artists than our art. Even if our own creative work flourishes, we miss out on so much if we don't offer the same love and careful attention to others' "art-children" that we do our own. And, unlike our creative work—work that is quite visible, and necessarily so—our servant-artistry of the soul on behalf of others is characterized by the credo "Don't let the left hand know what the right hand is doing." In other words, if you broadcast the personal things you've done for others, you've already gotten your reward. And it remains right here on plain old bankrupt earth.

Here's your opportunity to go for the gold: One of the fine arts of the soul is learning how to quietly—and privately—delight the heart of God.

That's a pleasure you can bank on.

Caring for one another's lives and work doesn't mean we're supposed to meet the spiritual and artistic needs of everyone who asks us for something. Jesus didn't meet every need he saw—and we're not called to do that, either. (Nor could we anyway, no matter how confident some of us might be in our brilliant talent for co-dependence.) What is true of Jesus, however, is that every need that he *did* meet . . . eventually became a story about *him*.

As artists of the soul, may we share the same holy privilege: May every need we meet for one another . . . simply become yet another story about Jesus.

CREATIVE MEDITATION: *Where the spirit of love is shed abroad in the heart, where the divine nature comes to full birth, where Christ the meek and lowly Lamb of God is truly formed within, there is given the power of a perfect love that forgets itself and finds its blessedness in blessing others.*

—ANDREW MURRAY, *Humility*

17

CLEAR AS MUD

When power corrupts, poetry cleanses.

—JOHN F. KENNEDY

*P*oetry is often seen as a luxury, an obscure art form for the esoteric. A language as clear . . . as mud. Yet Jesus himself was a poet—and he was anything but esoteric. Mysterious, yes—but not snobbish. So if you haven't read much poetry, there's no need to be intimidated by it. You can always draw encouragement from the example of the One whose head was so far in the clouds that his feet were firmly tethered to the ground.

There are a number of poets writing today who weave elegant strands of glint-grace throughout their work—poetry that shimmers with silver-chaliced promise, with the allure of Christ's presence. Some of these poets find sacred communion with the common elements of the world: dry flakes of leaves, a milk-rimmed, empty cereal bowl, a child's shame-faced performance at a Christmas pageant. Still others provide a clear-paned glimpse into their stained heart-struggle to flee from God, to leave behind the tattered vestments of a faith they're no longer quite sure of.

One of the best ways to begin reading poetry is simply to immerse yourself in it, even if its waters feel too deep—and see where poetry's undercurrents tow you. You may want to start with some poets whose works swirl with subtle (or not-so-subtle) faith (or lack of faith) themes: Susan Bergman, Wendell Berry, Scott Cairns, Michael Chitwood, David Citino, Annie Dillard, Diane

Glancy, Donald Hall, Geoffrey Hill, Andrew Hudgins, Julia Kasdorf, Jane Kenyon, John Leax, Kathleen Norris, Mary Oliver, Eric Pankey, Paul Mariani, James McAuley, Walter McDonald, Les Murray, Luci Shaw, Paul Willis. Of course, this is a shortlist—but these poets will get your feet wet.

In addition, both the poems and essays of the late Denise Levertov provide illuminating interior journeys for poets of the heart. Her mind-meets-soul verbal meanderings are stunningly provocative (try reading "What the Figtree Said"—a revealing poem written from the persona of the fig tree Jesus cursed). Her work is a good example of how poetry—with its condensed imagery and verbal mystery—can make things both more mysterious and yet more comprehensible than ever. Kind of like Jesus' parables.

Another wonderful contemplative poet is the Canadian writer Margaret Avison, now in her eighties. Avison, twice winner of Canada's Governor-General Award for poetry, is widely known in her own country for her faith-drenched work. And perhaps one of the best ways to explore Avison's unique skill for reducing a larger theme to its concise essence is to read an anything-but-poetic passage of Scripture.

In 1 Corinthians 3, Paul gives the church a sorely needed rhetorical dressing down. People are taking sides between two of God's servants—and Paul thinks they're all being big babies about it: "When one of you says, 'I'm on Paul's side,' and another says, 'I'm for Apollos,' aren't you being totally infantile?" he snorts.

"Who do you think Paul is, anyway? Or Apollos, for that matter? Servants, both of us—servants who waited on you as you gradually learned to entrust your lives to our mutual Master. We each carried out our servant assignment. I planted the seed, Apollos watered the plants, but God made you grow" (vv. 4–7 *The Message*).

Paul dismantles this divisive drama for what it is: spiritual immaturity. In God's kingdom, he says, there's no reason for such juvenile competitiveness. We're all on the same ball club. So whenever we see such rivalries brewing, let the umpire, the Holy Spirit, call them what they are: foul. And let's live them for what they are: There's only one side for the artist of the soul—and that's Christ's.

Margaret Avison's poetic reminder of this important spiritual truth provides a good dip into some of the clearer—yet more mysterious—waters of poetry:

THE JO POEMS
Josephine (Siggins) Grimshaw

Taking sides against destructiveness
brings on the very evil of destructiveness
unless it is clear that
no two persons
will or should
entirely agree,

i.e.

one must so take sides.
As clear as the mud she describes, eh?

CREATIVE EXERCISE: *Try reading a poet who intrigues you this week. More mysterious? What about writing a poem?*

18

THE PLEASURABLE ART OF PRAYER

The essence of all art is to have pleasure in giving pleasure.
—MIKHAIL BARYSHNIKOV

Jesus didn't just draw the line—he was master of the bottom line. He boiled the messy, hard-and-fast riff-raff of religious details into simple spiritual truths we all can grasp. And apply.

For instance, when matters appear too knotted and complex, Jesus nicely unravels them. Take the subject of prayer. "Here's what I want you to do," Jesus says. "Find a quiet, secluded place so you won't be tempted to role-play before God. Just be there as simply and honestly as you can manage. The focus will shift from you to God, and you will begin to sense his grace.

"The world is full of so-called prayer warriors who are prayer-ignorant. They're full of formulas and programs and advice, peddling techniques for getting what you want from God. Don't fall for that nonsense. This is your Father you are dealing with, and he knows better than you what you need. With a God like this loving you, you can pray very simply" (Matt. 6:7–8 *The Message*).

As Jesus says, when you know God loves you, you don't need to spend money learning complicated formulas in order to pray to him. Just get alone and talk to him. One on one. This kind of simple praying is an act of faith. It means you believe in the one you're praying to. The bottom line, Jesus says, is that if you're adding bells and whistles, then maybe you're not sure he's really listening.

Art is like prayer. All we need to do is to get alone and sit there "as simply and honestly as we can manage"—and do our thing. Create. Yet we often second-guess an uncomplicated process more than a complex one. There are times we think we need to add one more detail, one more sentence—because our creation felt too effortless in its birthing. Believe it or not, sometimes we struggle more with bearing a yoke that's easy than we do with laboring under the burden of hard-and-fast rules.

Art, like prayer, is really more about our giving pleasure to God than our performing for God. To delight in God—to focus solely on his pleasure—is to worship him. And worship is the true vocation of the artist of the soul. If we simply "do art as worship" the way Jesus encourages us to "do prayer," it's surprisingly easy. And in a world that's constantly telling us to work harder at everything, including our spiritual lives, that's a relief.

Those who worship God through creating art can allow themselves to be caught up, to be *unselfconscious*. To revel in the soul-blinding joy of knowing that the God of glory inhabits the art-praise of his people. To lift up hard-working heart-hands, and to say with delight, "This is what I made for you, Art-lover of mine." And after that, when you marvel at the work of his fingers—the iced moon and crackling stars and all that he has created—to be soul-stunned at the wonder that he's always mindful of *you*.

To worship God—to enjoy him—while creating is an act of faith. When, like prayer, you put aside the desire to role-play and come quietly, expectantly, he wants you to know he listens. He hears. He knows why you're sitting at that potter's wheel, that sewing machine, that kitchen table. And he delights when you delight in him.

Art—and the art of the soul—is allowing simple things to be simple, and hard things to be hard. Prayer and artful worship are easy things.

That's Jesus' bottom line. What a pleasure.

SCRIPTURE MEDITATION: *"Are you tired? Worn out? Burned out on religion? Come to me. Get away with me and you'll recover your life. I'll show you how to take a real rest. Walk with me and work with me—watch how I do it. Learn the unforced rhythms of grace. I won't lay anything heavy or ill-fitting on you. Keep company with me and you'll learn to live freely and lightly"* (Matt. 11:28–30 *The Message*).

19

How to Be the
"Low Man" on the Totem Pole

*St. Teresa described our life in this
world as like a night at a second-class hotel.*

—MALCOLM MUGGERIDGE

For over half a century, Arthur Miller's play *Death of a Salesman* has loomed as a theatrical monument to the human casualties of America's love affair with success. The lead character in the play, a traveling salesman named Willy Loman, lives in a desperate fantasy world. Since he has not achieved his own dream of greatness, Willy wagers the entire sum of his hopes on his two struggling adult sons, Biff and Happy, who continually disappoint him. The entire play traces Willy's tawdry life, his slow downward spiral, until, at the end, we are quite certain what the tragic result will be.

In a *New Yorker* article, Arthur Miller describes how he came up with the name "Willy Loman" for his protagonist. In Fritz Lang's 1933 film *The Testament of Dr. Mabuse,* a group of forgers chase and humiliate the detective who has worked to apprehend them. We see the detective crying into the phone to his former boss, "Lohmann? Help me, for God's sake!" The very next scene shows the detective, now in a hospital gown in an asylum, yelling into an imaginary phone, "Lohmann? Lohmann? Lohmann?"

"What the name really meant to me," Miller explains, "was a terrified man calling into the void for help that will never come."

Even the playwright's choice of the name "Willy Loman" was designed to enhance the darkness and despair of the piece.

Some years ago, a newspaper reporter asked Miller if his writing was based mainly on philosophical ideas on characters. "I'm not sure the theater cures people. I'm not sure it's important politically," Miller began. "What you can do is lay open the fundamental wages of sin—to use the Bible—to say, 'Now this is what you're up to, people.' Hopefully, you educate. 'Know the truth and it will make you free' . . . ."

In other words, *Death of a Salesman* is an American stage-study of Romans 6:23a: "The wages of sin is death."

There is a particular courage and stark beauty found in art that dares to tackle this subject of sin. Usually, however, those works aren't attached to the names of professing Christians. Many believing artists find it easier—and less costly, less controversial—to err on the glorious B-side of the Romans verse: "But the gift of God is eternal life in Christ Jesus our Lord."

Want to see a memorable picture of the wages of unforgiveness? Watch Merchant and Ivory's *Howard's End*. Want to see a heartbreaking portrayal of self-deception? Mike Leigh's *Secrets and Lies*.

A story is told of Henrik Ibsen, whose plays offended the moralists of his day. When someone compared Ibsen to Zola, a naturalist, he protested vehemently. "Zola descends into the cesspool to take a bath," Ibsen said. "I, to cleanse it."

There is a risk to artists who would create such works of art. Their work may be seen—and denounced—as being more like Zola's decadent descent into the cesspool, rather than like Ibsen's claimed internal motive to purify. That's why an artist's prophetic vision is paramount if he or she is going to get down and dirty and create such works.

A similar situation is discussed in the Bible, when the prophet Samuel is given the task of anointing the next king of Israel. As the first promising candidate stands in front of him, Samuel thinks to himself, "He must be the one." But God intervenes with his perspective on the matter. "The LORD does not look at the things man looks at," God says. "Man looks at the outward appearance, but the LORD looks at the heart" (1 Sam. 16:7 NIV). Eventually the Lord tells Samuel to anoint David, youngest of the eight sons of Jesse—not even in the starting lineup paraded before the prophet.

As God instructed the prophet Samuel, the prophetic artist won't be able to use logic alone to try to create something that will be "anointed." Rather, he or she will need to be carefully attuned to the desires of the God who doesn't pay much attention to outward appearances—the God who often goes straight to the heart of the sin-matter, as Arthur Miller did in creating *Death of a Salesman.*

If you truly believe, as the playwright did, that the truth will set us free—then go ahead and tell it. As a result, you may be low man on the religious totem pole. Yet the cost you pay as an artist of the soul is nothing less than the true wages of freedom—both yours and your audience's.

So why not be courageous like that American playwright Arthur Miller—and dare to point the bony finger of prophetic truth at all of our hearts?

PRAYER: *Lord, help me to explore new avenues of courageous creativity—to find new ways of expressing your truth in the world. Give me a bold, prophetic vision for the arts.*

20

ORCHESTRATING BLIND DATES

*A master and a maverick
make beautiful music together.*

—*THE NEW YORKER*, OCTOBER 19, 1998

*I*f you were to time-travel back to the music geography of the seventies, you'd stumble upon some musical collaborations that, well, just seem to make sense: Sonny and Cher, Hall and Oates, The Captain and Tennille. They make sense because we remember them as likely duos, likely singing partners. They seemed as though they went better together as collaborators than any way we could imagine them as solo artists.

It's this sort of assumption that makes a recent collaborative effort so unique: Two solo artists—one from the sixties, one from the seventies—teamed up as a most unlikely duo . . . and produced a head-spinner of an album. "Painted from Memory" is the result of the pairing of Burt Bacharach, love-song guru ("What the World Needs Now is Love, Sweet Love") and Elvis Costello, punk, new-wave icon of "Watching the Detectives." A combination, you might think, that's as likely as pairing the Partridge Family and the Clash. Put them onstage together and you'd get at the very least a fashion disaster: white-patent-leather-shoes-with-chains meet black-leather-jacket-with-chains.

Actually, at first, it was hard to get both Bacharach and Costello in the same room together—yet only for logistical reasons. A few years before the release of "Painted from Memory," Bacharach and

Costello wrote a song together, "God Give Me Strength"—collaborating entirely by fax and answering machine. Out of this long-distance writing process grew a mutual desire: Both were curious to continue exploring the possibilities of their somewhat strange musical partnership.

Bacharach describes the beginning stages of the collaborative process: "It's always like a blind date. The first time you go out, you don't know how it's going to be to sit in a room with them." But after getting together in the recording studio for the first time, both Bacharach and Costello knew that their musical styles should continue "dating."

Here lies one more wonder of the body of Christ: Our collaborative work as the church often appears as strange as the teaming of Burt Bacharach with Elvis Costello. Sometimes when two or more of us gather in Jesus' name, we resemble nothing more than a mismatched blind date. Our pairings can seem unlikely: green-grassy-lawn-watering yuppies singing hymns and choruses with green, grassy-haired youth. Pot-roast-cooking grandmas praying alongside former pot-smoking hippies.

The apostle Paul celebrates every such unlikelihood. "A body isn't just a single part blown up into something huge," he says. "It's all the different-but-similar parts arranged and functioning together" (1 Cor. 12:14 *The Message*). Just as Burt Bacharach and Elvis Costello are similar through the broad bond of musicianship, so we individuals in the church are similar through our shared bond of Christ. Yet within this bond, God frequently gets wildly creative:

He connects a trilling, bejewelled Bacharach hand with a stomping, black-booted Costello foot.

And here is where the true beauty and mystery of God's work in the world occurs—not in what seems predictable but in what seems beyond the limits of our own imaginations. The wonder of the body of Christ is that each person, as unique as his or her particular "musical" style might be, has a much-needed place in the orchestra of God. And the most gorgeous collaborations can come from the pairings of the most unlikely people.

When you're a part of such incredible musical orchestration, nothing is beyond the realm of creative possibility. Especially relationship. And, oftentimes, the stranger the pairing, the better the music. You know that woman in your church who wears a bee-hive hairdo that would've made Dusty Springfield envious? Think Bacharach. When you need it most, she might just know the way to San Jose. And that teenager in your youth group who wears Roy Orbison glasses—but adamantly insists to you that Austin Powers invented them? Think Costello. Like God, he often makes cameo appearances—and often shows up in the most unlikely places, under the most unlikely circumstances.

It doesn't matter whether musicians are old masters or young mavericks—they're always ripe for creativity, for new and unique collaborations. That's because they *love* music. Likewise, whenever we're most passionate about our Music, then we're most ready for the surprising blind dates of the Spirit.

Through the common bond of the music of Christ, we artists of the soul can fit together like . . . Burt Bacharach and Elvis Costello

PRAYER: *God, please open my eyes and ears to the strange collaborations you're orchestrating right now in my life—and through your church.*

21

A CLASSIC CASE

> *A classic is classic not because it*
> *conforms to certain structural rules, or fits*
> *certain definitions (of which its author had quite*
> *probably never heard). It is classic because of*
> *a certain and irrepressible freshness.*

—EZRA POUND

*I*n 1991, *New York* magazine film critic David Denby wrote his way through an unusual midlife passage. A journalist since he'd graduated from Columbia University, Denby had critiqued film regularly for more than twenty years. But, as he recalls, "by the early nineties I was beginning to be sick at heart." Not from films or film criticism, he explains, but from what the French philosopher Guy Debord calls "the society of the spectacle"—the soul-drain of living in a media-based culture. Denby found himself growing increasingly dissatisfied with "the incredible activity and utter boredom, the low hum of needs being satisfied."

But not *his* needs, Denby realized.

The critic longed to experience a sense of solidity, a deeper sense of reality amidst the quicksand of popular culture. As he says, "I possessed information without knowledge, opinions without principles, instincts without beliefs." It was time for a drastic change.

Denby chronicles the process of that change in *Great Books: My Adventures with Homer, Rousseau, Woolf, and Other Indestructible Writers of the Western World.* Thirty years after he first attended

Columbia University, the forty-eight-year-old film critic re-enrolled in the same two core classes he was required to take in 1961—Literature Humanities and Contemporary Civilization. He went back to school with eighteen-year-old freshmen and, once again, studied classic literature—Dante, Aristotle, Shakespeare, Nietzsche, the Bible. And Denby says he emerged from this experience with a fresh, new, compelling view of his world—and himself.

One of the film critic's many personal revelations occurs when a professor discusses the New Testament, particularly the person of Jesus Christ. Denby, a Jew, tells what he gained by his professor's admonition to read "selfishly"—to read in order to build a self. Christ becomes part of Denby's new selfhood, a figure who helps him reflect honestly on the hazards of middle age:

"[W]hen someone who is not a Christian reads the Passion story, what strikes him most strongly is Jesus' extraordinary presence of mind, his strength and shrewdness as well as sweetness, and his toughness, which at times is stunning. . . . Oh, I loved my Jesus! And I feared him, too. . . . The middle age 'success'—one of Jesus' prime targets—relied on his strengths, hid his weaknesses, and cut corners whenever he could; he observed the outward forms of the law and wondered what was alive in his soul."

Later, in the second semester, Dante's *Inferno* erupts as yet another doorway for Denby to explore the mysteries of the Christian faith. His professor invites the students to create their own version of hell, using Dante's prototype: The sinful pleasure indulged in during this life becomes its own punishment in the life to come. Surprisingly, Denby finds himself growing impatient with his fellow students' misinterpretations of Dante: "They believed in ethics, not in sin," he says, "and so they constructed a politically correct hell in which intolerance and ignorance were the worst offenses."

Throughout his year-long journey reading well-loved classic literature, Denby discovered that he could once again explore, ponder, ask questions. He could return to a state of intellectual wonder. "The courses in the Western classics force us to ask all those questions about self and society we no longer address without embarrassment—the questions our media-trained habits of irony have tricked us out of asking," he says. "In order to ask those questions, students need to be enchanted before they are disenchanted. They need to love the text before they attack the subtext."

Perhaps reading classic literature could help change us—and our art—just as it did David Denby. Perhaps it could invite us to ask deeper questions rather than reflexively spout superficial answers. Even teach us to create works of art that actively engage the souls—and actions—of our readers or viewers, instead of encouraging them to listen to our culture's insistent "low hum of *needs being satisfied.*"

Perhaps reading classic literature—including the Bible—could ignite our hearts to love the Text, as David Denby says, before we attack the cultural subtext.

CREATIVE SPIRITUAL EXERCISE: *Start today. It's not too late. Whom haven't you read? Shakespeare? Jane Austen? Or maybe it's St. Augustine or Teresa of Avila or Simone Weil. Or Leviticus. Whoever or whatever it is, why not create a year-long reading list? Or, sign up for a classic literature course at a local college.*

22

"AND THE OSCAR FOR BEST DISCIPLE IN A SUPPORTING ROLE GOES TO . . ."

Art is too serious to be taken seriously.

—AD REINHARDT

One of the most—if not *the* most—famous paintings of all time portrays a woman smiling slightly, looking as if she might be hiding an amusing secret. The painting, of course, is *Mona Lisa,* painted by Leonardo da Vinci. Yet this artistic work is also known by another name: *La Gioconda*—the joking one. It's a supreme irony that one of the most serious subjects of art scholars throughout the ages is a painting about a woman cracking jokes. Yet it also seems so . . . perfect. So . . . biblical.

That's right: There are passages in the Bible where, if you use your imagination to enter the scene portrayed, it's hard to keep yourself from laughing. For instance, this hilarious episode of biblical errors:

In Mark 10:35–41, the disciples James and John (who, up to this point in Jesus' story, seem fairly sane and level-headed), approach Jesus with a simple request. They ask, "Teacher, we want you to do whatever we ask of you." Now that's chutzpah. You can almost picture Jesus, slightly amused, as he asks them straight-faced, "And what do you want me to do for you?" Tell me guys. Your wish is my command. Or, at least, you probably think it is.

Theirs is a most humble proposition: "Grant that we may sit in your glory, one on your right, and one on your left." Can you imagine? In other words, "We'd like joint Oscars for best disciples in a supporting role." Hollywood marketers take note: They bypassed the Academy and went straight to Price-Waterhouse, the Source of the ballot-counting. They wanted to be kings of the *kingdom*—a request much bigger and badder than merely "kings of the world." (This loud and flashy demand makes their nickname "Sons of Thunder" seem highly appropriate.)

But it gets worse. Jesus respectfully answers them. "I'm afraid you don't really know what you're asking for. Are you able to drink the cup that I drink, or to be baptized with the baptism with which I am baptized?"

That's when you can picture them solemnly looking at Jesus, then one another, then finally back to Jesus. Their earnest response is recorded for all time:

"Oh, we are able," they say.

Right.

Think of the great punch lines Jesus could have delivered here. Instead, he patiently explains to them why he can't grant their request (while the other disciples blow a spiritual gasket at their swaggering bravado). Leave it to Jesus to turn this comedy of errors into a beautiful object lesson on servanthood. He kindly proceeds to explain that the kingdom of God operates in an entirely different manner than the world does. Don't be caring about the Oscar, he says. Care about the ostracized. Care about one another.

For the soul-artist, laughter is a gift—most especially when we can freely, joyfully laugh at ourselves. One of the greatest signs of humility is the giggle of grace and the gut-grinding of repentance, all in one, enlightened moment. You have to wonder if James and John ever looked back at that ridiculous moment and laughed: *Lord, how foolish. Lord, forgive me.*

One translation of the word "blessed" in the Bible is "silly." Silly are the poor in spirit (those who don't have it together spiritually), for theirs is the kingdom of heaven. Silly are the pure in heart, for they shall see God. Artists of the soul are the silly ones who follow a God who can set us free from the suffocating burden of taking ourselves—and our art—too seriously.

When you're suffering from a bad case of over-solemnity, remember that one of the finest and most venerated paintings ever painted, the *Mona Lisa*, portrays a woman cracking jokes. And one of the finest passages in the entire Bible on kingdom living is found in the midst of an amusingly bad *Saturday Night Live* skit—acted out by two wild and crazy guys who look just like us at times.

PRAYER: *God, teach me humility in my life and art: Help me to laugh at myself. Show me when I'm taking myself too seriously, and lead me into the grace of your "silly" joy.*

23

Playing Musical Chores

*All art constantly aspires
toward the condition of music.*

—WALTER PATER

The pianist Arthur Rubenstein recounts his first professional rehearsal experience with the legendary conductor Toscanini. The orchestra was performing the Beethoven C Minor Concerto, and the pianist was extremely nervous. As the first movement ended, however, Rubenstein was no longer nervous—he was *horrified.* He and the conductor had plowed through totally different interpretations of the piece. "Is this the great Toscanini?" the pianist thought. Their collaboration was a musical disaster.

The conductor then turned to Rubenstein and asked if he planned on playing the first movement as he'd played it the first time around. The pianist said yes, and Toscanini motioned for the orchestra to begin the piece again, from the top.

"And then—the miracle!" Rubenstein says. "While I had been playing, Toscanini had been listening. He had memorized every tempo I had used, every one of my phrasings, every expression mark. On the repetition it was though we had played the music together all our lives." The conductor had quietly studied the pianist's style while continuing to direct in his own unique fashion. He then returned to the piece—and this time he led the orchestra in the pianist's interpretation. In order to best capture Rubenstein's vision, Toscanini had lost all inhibitions about the concerto's sound the first time around.

Conductors, editors, publishers, film directors, teachers, patrons—they're indispensable figures in the art world. And a particular type of creativity characterizes these people who are called to lead or direct artists. They not only understand and appreciate a particular art form (whether music or writing or drawing); they know both how to intuit an artist's true style and how to orchestrate what's necessary for that gift to flourish and shine. Yet something else is required of these leaders: a creative, uninhibited vision for the *purpose* of good art—a vision that often transcends the "first movement" of the mainstream art industry.

An editor at a religious publishing house once spoke on what he calls "the prophetic role of the publisher." This editor believes that, every year, a publishing house should publish one or two books that are *needed,* rather than merely *wanted*—not necessarily best-selling titles, but books that deeply nourish the mind and soul. Obviously, in order to maintain such a standard, a publisher would need to "pull a Toscanini"—it would need to shake off some of its financial inhibitions while learning to intuit the rhythm and tempo of the Artist. And, like Toscanini, it would need to be prepared for its creative venture's beginnings to look incredibly foolish.

This editor's words are a good reminder to all of us in the creative process: Artists take risks, yes—but those who help develop, lead, and produce artists often take even greater risks.

In the Book of Hebrews, we're instructed on how to treat those who take the eternal risk of leading us in the spiritual finesse of the art of the soul: "Appreciate your pastoral leaders who gave you the Word of God," the author says. "Take a good look at the way they live, and let their faithfulness instruct you, as well as their truthfulness.

"Be responsive to your pastoral leaders. Listen to their counsel. They are alert to the condition of your lives and work under the strict supervision of God. Contribute to the joy of their leadership, not its drudgery. Why would you want to make things harder for them?" (Heb. 13:7, 17 *The Message*).

These faithful shepherds who conduct us in the orchestra of the body of Christ have a huge job. After all, this life is really nothing more than a continual "first movement"—as our leaders learn to listen to the Spirit's rhythms in order to direct the work of the church. Yet we have to remind ourselves we're engaged in a trial run: The music we produce together as God's symphony often sounds like bad Christian cacophony. And if we don't know what we're hearing—or why we're hearing it—it's easy for us to want to quit the band.

Yet artists of the soul are called to offer something different: a sympathetic understanding—and vision—of our leaders' purpose in directing the first movement. As with Toscanini, their purpose is not to get it *right,* it's to get *in tune.* If the conductors we know desire both to hear the Music and to see it richly expressed in the world, we're to offer them our respect and appreciation—even if their *staccato* sometimes clashes with our *legato.*

As artists, we can consciously seek to support—in any way we can—the producers, editors, and directors we know who are taking creative and financial risks to promote good art. And, in the same way, we artists of the soul can seek to encourage the faithful conductors of the Spirit among us—those who take the spiritual risk of leading us, in order that the Music might resound around the world.

CREATIVE SPIRITUAL EXERCISE: *Who are the Toscaninis you know—those who lead you spiritually? Artistically? Take some time this week to pray for their encouragement.*

24

WHEN GOD THROWS
THE BOOK AT YOU

*Art, like morality, consists
in drawing the line somewhere.*

—G. K. CHESTERTON

The Ten Commandments appear as straightforward and solid as the stone tablets they were written on: Do not murder. Do not steal. Do not commit adultery. The commandments are God's daily "don't do" (rather than "to do") list. Simple and concrete. Yet could it be there is more mystery, more poetry—perhaps even more responsibility—swimming fluidly beneath the seeming granite of those words? A Polish film director, Krzysztof Kieslowski, thought so.

Kieslowski, who died just a few years ago, is best known to American audiences for his film trilogy *Blue, White,* and *Red.* The director took a unique risk in 1988 by producing *Decalogue,* a ten-part cycle of short films for Polish television that, as *Time* says, "may be the great film achievement of the past decade." In *Decalogue,* Kieslowski sculpts the rock-solid tablets of the Ten Commandments' words into muddy, clay human beings—people who either keep or break those words in ways that powerfully disrupt our concrete vision.

In *Decalogue 1* ("Thou shalt have no other gods before me"), we meet a math professor who possesses immense confidence in the infallibility of his computer calculations. Everything is explainable, understandable, measurable. The professor's logical personality is highlighted by the fact that his eleven-year-old son, Pawel, is curious about many subjects—particularly the more difficult matters of God and death. When the boy wants to try out his new pair of ice skates at a local pond, the two of them consult the father's source for irrefutable information. The computer's data—calculating weather, temperature, etc.—is sure: The ice is sturdy enough to hold the boy's weight. What happens from that point on is, as you might guess, the tragic result of the father's forgetfulness of the first commandment. And it raises an interesting question: When does our reliance upon the created world—including the things we fashion with our hands, minds, spirits—subtly cross over into the shadowland of idolatry?

Decalogue 7 ("Thou shalt not steal") twists its way through even more confusing questions. We meet Ania, a six-year-old girl brought up to believe that her grandmother, Ewa, is her mother—and that her real mother, Majka, is her older sister.

The web of secrets and lies stems from family shame: When Majka was a schoolgirl, she had an affair with her teacher and became pregnant. Ewa fiercely took over the role of mother she would assume for years. Yet, over time, the charade has begun to unravel. Majka is now desperate for Ania to love her as a mother, and she finally kidnaps the child, seeking refuge with her former lover, Wotjek.

Yet Ewa will not be deterred from claiming what she believes is both her right to Ania, her granddaughter—and Majka, her real daughter. She searches everywhere for them. As the ending of this sad drama unfolds, we wonder: Who has really stolen from whom in this film? And haven't we all, at some time, stolen in the ways we see these characters stealing from one another?

Neither Kieslowski nor his screenwriter, Krzystof Piesiewicz, admitted to practicing an active faith. Both were more intrigued about exploring what they saw as an old-style morality in a Catholic country intersecting with the modern age. Yet through their unorthodox vision, *Decalogue* offers a rare combination: simple, eternal, granite truths mixed with real, fleshy, very human complexities—a lethal combination that can only lead us into deeper questions. And deeper answers as well.

The creative soul knows that growing spiritually involves more than a rote recitation of the rules. It embraces an unfolding, panoramic vision of God—and a recognition of the daily, eternal drama in which we each live. In the art of the soul, "Do not steal" does not merely translate as "Do not swipe pens from the office, shoplift at Target, rob the Wells Fargo truck." It also means, "Do not rob the joy of others when they celebrate. Do not grab the precious parts of people's souls and peddle them as if they were your own creations. Do not steal your friends' delight by refusing to create the gift of beauty you could hand them if you weren't so afraid of failure."

There is a unique responsibility attached to the word "artist." It is always to give more—see more, create more, love more— than what is merely required. The bottom line for the artist is not merely truth, but truth *and* love. Truth *and* beauty. It takes an unswerving love for the Poet of the Commandments to swallow the truth of his tablet-words, then allow them to run liquid and living—and beautiful—through our souls.

As an artist of the soul, you're not off the creative hook—even when you live by the book.

CREATIVE EXERCISE: *Choose one of the commandments to meditate on this week. Think about ways to refresh its meaning in your life. You might even want to create an interpretative work of art: a dance, poem, painting, line drawing.*

25

THE NOT-SO-HAPPILY-EVER-AFTER SCREENPLAY

*Of all that is written,
I love only what a person has written
with his own blood.*

—FRIEDRICH NIETZSCHE

*I*f Nietzsche truly believed what he says above, then you wonder what he thought of the blood-and-guts writing of the psalmists. For those of us who like neat, tidy views of faith, the Psalms provide a good, healthy dose of reality. David, the best-known psalmist, was definitely a Disneyland kind of guy: He liked to ride roller-coasters. Big, scary ones. In the anguish-strewn prayers of the Psalms, we watch him dance wildly one moment and weep in despair the next. This "man after God's own heart" comes across as a flaming manic depressive.

Psalm 88, in particular, offers us a bleak, black-and-white snapshot of David's despair. The Psalm itself does not have a happy ending. There is no pink Cadillac with fins heading into the sunset with David sipping a chocolate milkshake. In fact, the thought he ends with seems pretty hopeless: "Thy burning anger has passed over me; Thy terrors have destroyed me," he says. "They have surrounded me like water all day long; They have encompassed me altogether. Thou hast removed lover and friend far from me; My acquaintances are in darkness" (Ps. 88: 16–18 NASB). Whoa. No purple praise banners waving. No triumphant "we shall tread on scorpions" victory songs. No *Footprints* toodling tranquilly through the sand. Just harsh, ugly, desperate feelings.

A friend once wrote me a paraphrase of another part of this psalm: "Lord, do you like my praises, as you say you do? If so, Lord, think of this: The dead don't praise you, do they? No more me, no more of those praises you love, right? So Lord, if you love those praises, keep me alive—is that a deal, or what?" In my friend's paraphrase, David was so desperate, he even used his praises as a bribe for sanity.

Regardless of David's fears, God kept him alive. And David rose up to praise God in the land of the living. His poetry—his art—was not only a place to pour out those dark emotions. This broken, frightened man's poetry became part of the Holy Scriptures for all time.

Catherine Drinker Bowen says, "Writers seldom choose as friends those self-contained characters who are never in trouble, never unhappy or ill, never make mistakes, and always count their change when it is handed to them." Writing well includes developing full-bodied characters. And one of the best examples of this is the Bible—God's memory book of friends. They are among those who sometimes get in trouble, are unhappy or ill, make lots of mistakes, and give away all their loose change before they even count it. That exceptional poet, novelist, playwright, and screenwriter, God, chooses interesting characters for companions. And dark-hearted David was one of them.

Sometimes people avoid the art of the soul because they think they're going to have to clean themselves up before they come to the canvas. That they'll have to sanitize their poetry, censor their screenplays. That they'll have to make sure they learn a bunch of church rules and abide by them before they can attain the label "friend of God."

That's why David's "hopeless" poem, Psalm 88, is actually so hopeful. It tells the truth about both God and us. It tells us that God loves us no matter what kind of emotional basketcase we are. It tells us to bring our hearts—and our art—just as we are today, right now—and allow God to worry about what the ending to our saga is going to be.

Wherever you're at today, you can create—and live—right in that very space. Even if it feels empty, lonely, cramped, dark. God is the original author of the "not-so-happily-ever-after" screenplay. And He's one great script doctor. So, like David, you can take your heart out of the can when you're hurting and let it bleed unashamedly. That's good art. Good art for *the soul*.

CREATIVE MEDITATION: *[The soul in darkness] is like the traveler, who, in order to go to new and unknown lands, takes new roads, unknown and untried, and journeys unguided by his past experience . . . . Exactly so, one who is learning fresh details concerning any office or art always proceeds in darkness, and receives no guidance from his original knowledge, for if he left not that behind he would get no farther nor make any progress; and in the same way, when the soul is making most progress, it is traveling in darkness, knowing naught.*

—ST. JOHN OF THE CROSS, *Dark Night of the Soul.*

26

OBVIOUSLY

The best actors do not let the wheels show.

—HENRY FONDA

O ne of the greatest temptations of artists is, as Henry Fonda says so succinctly, letting the wheels show. That is, allowing the internal creative mechanisms, the creative driving force, to hang out for all the world to see. Fonda is talking about a kind of theatrics that draws attention to the process of acting itself, rather than a natural style that motors smoothly across the screen or stage. When the wheels show on an actor, we're conscious that what we're watching is acting—rather than observing a real person in a real story, speaking real words into his or her real world. And make no mistake: Fonda lived what he preached. If you've ever watched *On Golden Pond,* he's not spinning his wheels. He simply *was* Norman.

Henry Fonda's words of wisdom hold true across the disciplines, whether painting, writing, dancing, singing. Whenever we allow the wheels to show, we're headed for an artistic flat tire. And this kind of creative road-trip breakdown is a common occurrence among Christian artists. We're often known for turning our art—a vehicle of God—into a spiritual low-rider designed to draw attention to the wheels.

I'm talking about "obvious" art—art that doesn't reveal God naturally but that blares him out the windows of our souls like a bad eight-track player. Art draped with God-words and slogans and Bible verses like fuzzy dice hung on rearview mirrors. Art that doesn't just reveal the wheels, but that wears fluorescent hubcaps shouting, "God has hopped aboard my hovercraft—pay attention."

This isn't to say art that mentions God or Jesus or the Bible is always obvious. In fact, obvious art isn't really about externals. What we're talking about is a *spirit* behind the art, behind the creation. We're really talking about the difference between creating out of faith or creating out of fear.

An Oklahoma artist named Ron Bizzell creates colorful, collage journal covers from greeting cards, confetti, gold and silver metallic pieces. I first learned of his work while attending a craft show. I was drawn magnetically to Ron's booth not because of his subject matter, but because of the buoyant life that exudes from his art. Later, as Ron and I talked, I discovered that he is a man of faith— and he often custom-designs his journal covers from old photos or other precious memorabilia that people send him. Ron Bizzell's work is a great example of *the art of faith.*

Whenever we force our Christian message into our art, we create out of fear. We create out of unbelief. We say that God is not big enough, not powerful enough, to dwell in what he gives our hands and hearts to do. We tell the world that the Holy Spirit isn't lively enough, creative enough to speak to people in his own unique and very personal way through our art. When we load our particular artistic vehicle with extraneous "God material," we reveal we have no trust in our internal Engine. And that kind of art is bound to fail—because it's bound by fear.

Is your art bound to faith or to fear? A work that is obvious is fearful; a work that is effortless is faithful. For contemporary examples of Christian content-crammed art with nicely unobtrusive wheels, read Kathleen Norris's *The Cloister Walk* or *Amazing Grace:*

A Vocabulary of Faith (if you haven't already). Or take a look at Anne Lamott's *Traveling Mercies*. These are books whose art-travels rest solidly on their God-centered wheels. Yet each treads so lightly that, as we read, we can't help but realize we stand on holy ground. Theirs is not obvious Christian art; it's art that's obviously Christian.

"Everything that does not come from faith," says the apostle Paul, "is sin" (Rom. 14:23b NIV). In other words, whatever we do that doesn't emerge from a heart fully convinced of that action's beauty or purpose or meaning falls short of God's superb glory. And the artist who's anxiously compelled to tack on superfluous God-content to his or her work does not create out of faith, but out of sinful fear.

However, in the verse immediately preceding this one, Paul offers words of life that can fuel the work of any artist, no matter where you are in the journey: "Blessed is the man who does not condemn himself by what he approves" (v. 22b). Blessed is the artist who so believes in the unabashed approval of God that he or she can create art dripping with God's approval.

Obviously.

CREATIVE SPIRITUAL EXERCISE: *This week, take a "fearless" inventory: Journal honestly about what might cause your art—or your life—to be obvious. Do your "wheels show"? May the gift of God's approval invade all that you touch.*

27

AND THE BEAT GOES ON . . .

> *We look at the dance to impart*
> *the sensation of living . . . to energize the spectator*
> *into keen awareness of the vigor, the mystery, the humor,*
> *the variety, and the wonder of life. This is the*
> *function of the American dance.*
>
> —MARTHA GRAHAM

*P*rimitive Mysteries is one of choreographer and dancer Martha Graham's most moving—and faith-drenched— works of art. Heavily influenced by Native American and Spanish culture, the dance is a spare, understated tribute to the life of Mary, the mother of Jesus. *Primitive Mysteries* is separated into three distinct sections: "Hymn to the Virgin," "Crucifixion," and "Hosanna"—each portion of the dance portraying a different emotional aspect of Mary's pilgrimage. The Virgin, dressed in white, is accompanied by a chorus of twelve, blue-clad women dancers.

Graham originally danced the role of Mary in the piece, created in 1931. The choreographer used the simplest of gestures, of movement, to convey both the grief and the ecstasy of Mary's responses to Christ's life. During one especially meaningful section on the death of her Son, Mary stands motionless at center stage, her hands pressed hard against her head. The other dancers then represent the crown of thorns, hands on foreheads and fingers splayed. As the second movement of the dance ends, the women stand together quietly. Then all walk off stage in perfect unison to the sound of a heavy, rhythmic beat.

The photographer Barbara Morgan once noticed a small detail about this moment in the original production. She said, "Each member seems to walk because of the beat whereas Graham steps because the beat itself has forced her to move." Since the entire piece is designed to revolve around the person of Mary, this is a good example of how Graham's choreography so subtly—and stunningly—fulfills its artistic aim. The uniformity of the movement of the chorus is what highlights Graham's ever-so-slight, syncopated variation. And the tiny detail Morgan highlights is also a metaphor for the dance of our everyday lives—and the Dancer who choreographs us, the One "in whom we live and move and have our being."

The beauty of beauty is that it exists outside the walls of what we often call "creative." It is the bright, rounded scribbles outside the lines. Yet it is also found in purposeful uniformity. Beauty can exist in sharp, angular lines; in simple, stark silence; in women moving together in perfect unison—as designed by Graham to create the chorus dance in *Primitive Mysteries*.

Beauty can even be repetition, sameness—the long, clean, precise line of a split-rail fence on ranch property. But don't tell that to artists. Many artists fear fences. *Fences restrict us.* On the other hand, we can erect our own, personal concrete walls—laws, rules, regulations—to keep us from taking risks, from creating. (Either way, the issue here is one of control: We're the one calling the shots. We're in charge.)

But fences can be good. They provide boundaries. You know exactly where your land ends . . . and where someone else's begins. You can peer over them, glimpse new territories.

Jesus came to earth as a human being. And he also came as God. And we're not God. That is the exact place where the land of our own personal reign as prima ballerina ends . . . and Christ's rule of principal Choreographer begins. There is a simple, clean line of demarcation between him and us. But that boundary is a thing of marvel, of beauty. And so is our unanimous movement together as his chorus of dancers on earth.

"How good and pleasant it is," exults the psalmist, "when brothers live together in unity" (Ps. 133:1 NIV). That "dance of unison," like Martha Graham's chorus, can highlight the Dancer, the One who moves eternally as the Beat itself. As you know, his Beat goes on. And on. And on. But let's admit it: We don't. We all know how rare unity really is. Especially among artists, the most off-beat of the bunch.

But here's our hope: We're not simply artists, but artists of the *soul*—those called to an amazing dance called beauty. This kind of beauty sees the pursuit of concord and peace as sheer artistry, as a means to highlight the subtle (and not so subtle) gestures of the Dancer. Beauty may be clumsy, awkward, graceless—but it will still strap on those pink satin shoes and practice every day, refusing to lose hope in the arduous task of seeking to create what is lovely. Its heart leaps to nurture relationships that bear the mark of Christ's own choreography, of his intricate sense of intimate detail.

Uniformity for its own sake isn't good. But in a dance that critics once called "probably the finest single composition ever produced in America," Martha Graham choreographed perfect unison as the dance itself. And, to quote another Creator, "It was very good."

In this case, God *was* in the details.

PRAYER: *God, sometimes our relationships with one another seem like such hopeless artistic ventures. And yet our glimpses of your stunning choreography, leave us longing to dance with you—and one another—more gracefully. Help us regain our passion to love one another fervently, from the heart.*

28

CROSS PURPOSES

*I am convinced that
there is no great filmmaker who
does not sacrifice something.*

—FRANCOIS TRUFFAUT

lthough the late French film director Francois
Truffaut is best known for his lyrical, unconven-
tional role behind the camera (*The 400 Blows, The
Last Metro*), he also enjoyed working in other arenas of
the movie-making business. In fact, Steven Spielberg thought so much
of his work that, out of gratitude, he cast Truffaut as a sympathetic scientist in *Close Encounters of the Third Kind*. In addition, Truffaut was
also a scrupulous, insightful movie critic, publishing his pointed film
reviews in *Cahiers du Cinema* and *Arts* magazines.

Despite the sharp criticisms he often leveled, Truffaut was profoundly sensitive to filmmakers' growth processes—and to what he
felt was the true meaning of success in making movies. Once, in the
mid-1950s, he reviewed a talented director's artistically disappointing
film—a director who'd already been dubbed by others as a cinematic
failure. Truffaut presents an altogether different take on the filmmaker
and his offering: He says that failure is a special talent—and that "to
succeed is to fail."

Many believe, Truffaut explains, that the perfect film is one in
which all elements are carefully and equally balanced. But the filmmakers who do the best work, he contends, are those who are always

willing to sacrifice an element for the whole of the piece: "Renoir will sacrifice anything—plot, dialogue, technique—to get a better performance from an actor. Hitchcock sacrifices believability in order to present an extreme situation he has chosen in advance. Rossellini sacrifices the connection between movement and light to achieve greater warmth in his interpreters." And so on.

The films that truly succeed, Truffaut tells us, make artistic sacrifices—sacrifices that don't ensure the work's popular appeal, but that nevertheless add richness through creative risk. In other words, the best films aren't necessarily the well-balanced ones, but those that lean heavily on one particular element to achieve a certain creative texture.

Such is the call of the soul-artist. Jesus tells us that to be his disciples we must pick up our splintered cross of wood and follow him. And often, the sacrifices he asks for run counter to a culture that increasingly values self-help, self-achieved balance above all else: "Anyone who intends to come with me has to let me lead," Jesus remarks. "You're not in the driver's seat—I am. Don't run from suffering; embrace it. Follow me and I'll show you how. Self-help is no help at all. Self-sacrifice is the way, *my* way, to finding yourself, your true self. What good would it do to get everything you want and lose you, the real you?" (Luke 9:23–25 *The Message*).

Francois Truffaut's approach to film suddenly gives us a bigger lens on Christ's words, projecting God's perspective of our "self-help" in a wide-screen format. When the *achievement of balance* becomes the driving creative force in our lives, we've neglected to pick up our rough and hard-hewn cross—and in the process we've lost our soul's artistry. We've lost the Spirit's creative texture—the distinctive "zing!" that reveals the difference between a life that's Christian and *a life that is Christ's*.

Artists are often seen as notoriously off-balance. But picking up your cross doesn't mean consciously living off-kilter—to deliberately skip so hard to the beat of a different drummer that you knock everyone else down. Rather, picking up your cross means that Christ calls the shots—the way any film director would.

Sacrifice means different things to different people. For instance, sacrifice for you might mean studying Renaissance art history in Italy instead of becoming a missionary to Nairobi. (How does your seminary training fit into *that* picture?) Or your cross might be giving up your black beret and your strolls through the East Village in exchange for a Chevy van and picking up kids in a Minneapolis car pool. (Using your bathtub as a kitchen sink in your New York City walk-up was easy; it's hauling Winnie-the-Pooh backpacks that's hard.)

However, picking up your cross doesn't necessarily mean doing something you don't like to do. *It means allowing God to lead you into whatever he determines your cross, your sacrifice, is.* When Francois Truffaut says that a good film leans heavily on one creative element rather than aiming for balance, the director's words merely mirror one of Jesus' central truths:

Artists of the soul lean heavily on one Element—Christ—in order to find the sacrificial cross they are called to carry creatively and faithfully in the world.

PRAYER: *God, perhaps there are crosses in my life I've picked up that I should lay down, and crosses that I've laid down that I need to pick up. Show me what they are. Please call the shots—starting today.*

29

PROCESSING FOOD

> *God doesn't give people talents*
> *that he doesn't want them to use.*
>
> —IRON EAGLE

friend told me about a wonderful, small dinner party she attended. What made the evening special, she said, was not just the intimate conversations she had with close friends, or the fragrant smell of crisp apples and sharp cheddar cheese. It was the hostess' simple artistic touch to the dining room table, where the food was arranged.

She'd covered the table with plain, brown wrapping paper. Then, she'd taken a magic marker and had drawn individual arrows pointing to each item of food, labeling them to the side as she went. "Artichoke dip," said one. "Chips and salsa." "Veggie plate."

It was a small thing, said my friend, but it added such brightness, such warmth to the festivities. She left that night with a joyful, satisfied heart.

The art of food? One of the most creative ventures imaginable. And giftedness in culinary skills is an art form to be savored, as we would a fine painting.

The writer M. F. K. Fisher, who was a regular contributor to *House Beautiful* from 1944 to 1957, consistently whetted the American palate for the subject of eating and entertaining. She understood what it meant to relish the art of preparing food: "The man must try to understand what it is about making a curry or a bouillabaisse that lightens his wife's face and heart," Fisher said in 1948, back when the art studio of the kitchen was mainly the domain of women. She eventually authored twenty books on the creative joys of food.

M. F. K. Fisher, may your spirit live on: It's time the everyday chefs of the world kick down the doors of their humble pantries—and come out of the cooking closet. Doesn't it take more artistic skill, more sense of rhythm and timing, more perseverance, to create a work of food-art than virtually any other thing? After all, paintings last forever, but the food on the dining room table lasts just a few minutes. It takes a true sense of vision—and purpose—to consistently create disappearing art.

A lot of New Testament stories about Jesus center around food. He seemed to enjoy getting together and eating with his friends, or with the curious who'd invited him over for a dinner party. And then there's the story of Jesus' big company picnic:

In John 6, when 5,000 people turned out to listen to his recipe for knowing God, Jesus decided he'd feed the whole group. He took a little boy's five barley loaves and two fish, broke them and gave thanks, then passed them around to those lounging on the lawn. In the end, miraculously, there were twelve big baskets of fish and chips left over. It seems his food, unlike ours, never disappeared entirely.

The meal he served, however, was not just simply for the purpose of satisfying his friends' rumbling stomachs at lunchtime. It was a metaphor for Christ himself. Food was a continual theme, a dominant image in his poetry:

"I am the Bread of Life," he says. "Your ancestors ate the manna bread in the desert and died. But now here is Bread that truly comes down out of heaven. Anyone eating this Bread will not die, ever. I am the Bread—living Bread!—who came down out of heaven. Anyone who eats this Bread will live—and forever! The Bread that I present to the world so that it can eat and live is myself, this flesh-and-blood self" (John 6:48–51 *The Message*).

Anyone who eats of me, Christ is saying, sits down at the Dinner Table that never runs out of food. You're not just eating eggplant parmigiana that's here today and then gone quicker than tomorrow. You're not just eating freeze-dried survival supplies, like the manna the children of Israel gulped in the wilderness. When you taste me, Jesus says, you feast on the Food-art that will never disappear. You're tasting the very best Meal that ever was or is, forever and ever, starting now. Today. I am that Food you crave.

Is cooking one of your art forms? When it's joyfully offered as worship to God, you reflect to us the nourishing poetry of Christ. Believe this: Long after the china and silver are cleared, leftovers of the Spirit will remain in our hearts like loaves and fishes. When you lovingly break your bread in his name, you remind us again of the Metaphor: You bless in our presence the Meal that never disappears, the one Art that lasts forever.

PRAYER: *Bread of heaven, I break and bless my art in your presence. Multiply it. Allow those who taste of what I offer, to take, eat, remember you.*

30

The Hidden Chambers of Art

*The highest art is always the
most religious and the greatest artist
is always a devout person.*

—PROFESSOR BLACKIE

*N*ear the turn of the last century, a young Scotsman faced a difficult decision. A talented visual artist, poet, and musician, the young man had spent two years sharpening his drawing skills at the National Art Training School in London. When he graduated, he was awarded a scholarship to study in some of Europe's finest art centers. It seemed inevitable he would pursue his creative dreams. Instead, he turned the generous offer down—and eventually he became a minister.

This Scottish preacher wrote some powerful thoughts about his two overwhelming passions in life—Christ and art—and his desire to see them reconciled. What was needed in the world, he felt, was not simply the development of Christian artists. He saw a pressing need for ministers who immersed themselves in the world of art and spoke to its concerns through Christ's prism:

"The kingdom of the aesthetics lies in a groveling quagmire, half fine, half impure; there is a crying need for a fearless preacher of Christ in the midst of that kingdom, for a fearless writer, writing with the blood of Christ, proclaiming His claims in the midst of that kingdom, for a fearless lecturer above pandering to popular taste, to warn and exhort that all the kingdoms of this world are to become Christ's—that artists, poets and musicians be good and fearless Christians . . . .

"The duty of ministers is to instruct the people out of bigoted notions against art. It is for the man of God artist to enter this aesthetic kingdom and live and struggle and strain for its salvation and exaltation."

This same young preacher lived out his spiritual desire: He became both a faithful minister of God's Word, and—through the posthumous publication of his journals—a spiritually creative writer whose work touched not only artists, but artists of the soul as well.

His name was Oswald Chambers. And he's well known for giving his artistic utmost for God's highest good.

A thoughtful pastor and writer, Eugene Peterson, once said he believes every seminary should offer courses in literature. What a vision: Rural pastors immersing themselves in *Paterson,* William Carlos Williams's book-length poem about life in his New Jersey hometown. Seminary professors discussing Dante and Dickens and Dostoyevsky. Inner-city youth workers studying the plain-barrio-speak of poet Gary Soto or the haunting novels of Toni Morrison.

The idea is appealing—and so fitting in a postmodern age, in which story is a central medium of the culture. Yet Oswald Chambers envisioned a step even beyond this: He was writing about the calling of *minister-artists.* No line of demarcation. Those who not only bring the Bible to their art, or even art to the Bible, but seek to proclaim the good news of *Bible-art.*

In other words, separation of church and the state-of-art.

To find some good examples of Chambers' vision, we may have to travel back a few centuries—back when the world was teeming with gifted, God-breathing, glory-gulping artists. Minister-artists.

Like that fine clergyman poet God consistently collared, George Herbert. Or the equally fine Jesuit landrover and writer of the *Windhover*, Gerard Manley Hopkins. Then there's the twelfth-century Catholic nun Hildegard of Bingen—a hum-dinger musician, poet, artist, and actress. Need one more? Done—John Donne.

If you're not called to be a minister or youth worker or missionary or seminary professor or pastoral counselor, then by all means, don't feel compelled to head in that direction. Same goes for being an artist (however, I doubt that about you, since you're reading this book). But if both of these passions burn equally in your heart, you don't need to separate them. You're a minister-artist—and you're needed. Now more than ever. Art . . . for Art's sake. And the Word's sake.

Now, you ministry-minded folks wouldn't want to go and disappoint your old friend Oswald Chambers, would you?

CREATIVE MEDITATION:*A spiritually drained minister once came to Oswald Chambers, seeking advice. Chambers asked him what he liked to read, and the minister replied that he only read the Bible and books related to the Scriptures. Chambers then scribbled out a list of more than fifty books of various genres. "My advice to you," said Chambers, "is to soak, soak, soak in philosophy and psychology, until you know more of these subjects than you ever need consciously to think . . . . When people refer to a man as a 'man of one book,' meaning the Bible, he is generally found to be a man of multitudinous books, which simply isolates the one Book to its proper grandeur. The man who only reads the Bible does not, as a rule, know it or human life."*

31

BEAUTY'S PRAYER

> *Art washes away from*
> *the soul the dust of everyday life.*
> —PABLO PICASSO

The natural world's incarnational beauty continuously murmurs God's presence—and we are often the fumbling-but-eager listeners, ear to the clodded earth, catching bits and snatches of his ongoing conversation with us. Pilgrimaging through brushy pine forests, up crooked mountain trails, we follow a scent that allures us, intrigues us, sometimes frustrates us. God is so close—yet so far away. We see him all around us, every day—yet we don't. Or do we? Perhaps that question is why nature is a favorite subject of poets, artists, musicians: We're caught in the bear trap of our own desperate creations to capture beauty's fleeting moments. And when artists do capture those moments, God seems never nearer.

The poet Anne Porter is one such artist. Her collection *An Altogether Different Language: Poems 1934–1994* is a compilation of more than sixty years of tracing the familiar scent of the One who lingers in salt-whipped seas, glittering morning stars, and the rabble-rousing of robins, chattering away on the bare branch of a tree. Her work, briskly concise, is laced as well with her rich Franciscan religious tradition:

THERESE

Therese, your statue's in our parish church,
But when you were a child you crossed these mountains
And drank the clear rock-shattered mountain water
And picked the daisies in the soaring meadows

And crept like us, over the black ravines.
"I can fall only into God," you said.

Porter's work often uses aspects of nature to describe human frailties. For instance, she compares the onset of old age to "tiny maple leaves . . . curling like birds' feet round the frost." Her senses, saturated with the sight and smell and taste of God's presence in the natural world, consistently marry her own humanity to the divinity she glimpses.

Porter's life itself mirrors an unusual blend of both high art and yet astounding simplicity. She married the painter Fairfield Porter, and their circle of intimates included what's known as the "New York School of Poets"—the avant-garde artists of the 1950s: Frank O'Hara, Kenneth Koch, John Ashbery, and James Schuyler. Both the Porters' homes in Southampton and Maine were warm, nourishing havens for artist-friends. In fact, Anne remarked once that "Schuyler came to lunch one day and stayed eleven years."

Amid the continuous artistic hubbub, however, the poet and her husband raised five children—one of whom was mentally disabled. The ending of her memorial poem to her disabled son, Johnny, is a poignant prayer:

. . . And now you're home.
Now you're with Mary, whose starry veil you loved,
And of whom you said, "She won't get bored with my puns,"
And, "She won't mind if I touch her dress."
While your mother, who sometimes did
     get bored with your puns,
Cries here on earth

And asks you, now that you're one of the greatest,
To grant her a portion of your littleness.

Much of Anne Porter's work is composed of such humble, quiet prayers—whether stated outright or deftly layered beneath the words, like seashells just below the surface of wet sand. Her poetry is a beautiful example of the limitless metaphors of promise to be unearthed from the natural world. She's an artist who not only sees, but *prays* with what she sees.

You, too, can capture for us such Beauty that we are brought to our knees.

PRAYER:
A SHORT TESTAMENT

Whatever harm I may have done
In all my life in all your wide creation
If I cannot repair it
I beg you to repair it,

And then there are all the wounded
The poor the deaf the lonely and the old
Whom I have roughly dismissed

As if I were not one of them.
Where I have wronged them by it
And cannot make amends
I ask you
To comfort them to overflowing,

And where there are lives I may have withered around me,
Or lives of strangers far and near
That I've destroyed in blind complicity,
And if I cannot find them
Or have no way to serve them,

Remember them. I beg you to remember them

When winter is over
And all your unimaginable promises
Burst into song on death's bare branches.

—ANNE PORTER

32

THANK GOD, ART IS NOT GOD

> *What advantages are there for a writer*
> *in [having faith]? . . . He is saved from the*
> *romantic tendency toward idolatry. Art is not religion.*
> *A writer is not a god or godling. There is wisdom*
> *and illumination but not salvation in a sonnet.*
>
> —CHAD WALSH

The poetry reading that night had the distinct feel of a prestigious club. There were stuffy insider comments, aloof presentations. A solemn sense of self-importance and self-preservation permeated the place like waxy incense. In fact, the whole event reeked of the musty scent of . . . religion.

Religion always excludes, always has the effect of making us feel *lesser than*. Religion is a system of measurement that has an ending point of infinity. It offers the illusion of arrival—but once you reach the destination, it smiles sardonically and says, "By the way, you're not even halfway there yet." Religion is an elite society where the rules constantly change, in order to oppress you. Religion is counterfeit faith.

That's why artists who truly enter into the holy temple of Christ often feel like somersaulting and dancing a cheerful polka. Christ-artists are free. Christ-artists have no hoops to jump through, no punishing, exacting code to live up to. Instead, they enjoy a table of fresh bread and wine—one that nourishes their souls, sends them out from the feast and into the streets to feed and love and give. And to celebrate freedom.

Ragamuffin Christ-artists don't have to worship at the golden shrine of art. Instead they can enjoy art to the hilt—precisely because it is not God. Such artists are set free from the frenzy of pouring over Picasso or scrupulously studying Shakespeare or memorizing Molière for the purpose of finding truth. Instead, they know truth from the ordinary life of One who became simple, and because of that, are invited to discover him in every nook and cranny of Picasso, Shakespeare, Molière, and the endless company of the artists of the ages.

Ultimately, we hate what we idolize. Idols are like cheap baubles with deceptively expensive exteriors, like those fake designer watches sold on New York streets that fall apart the minute you wind them. As Paul says, those who buy into idols trade "the glory of God who holds the whole world in his hands for cheap figurines you can buy at any roadside stand" (Rom. 1:23 *The Message*). But, unlike those watches, idols aren't just an inconvenience. They are ruthless gods that exact a price from our souls.

The purpose of idols is to destroy our rollicking, holy enjoyment of God and one another. And, ironically, if we worship art, we're not free to enjoy even the thing we worship. We can't truly revel in the glory of grunge music when we depend upon it to save our souls. Only when it's not all-important are we free to love art passionately and to pursue the pure enjoyment of it.

We can fashion idols out of art, yes. But hold on. There's also a flip side to art-idolatry: We can likewise create an idol out of *hating* art. Fiction and films and paintings are often labeled tools of darkness, designed to taint our souls with their evil, poisonous tentacles. Art is to be feared, shunned, abhorred. Yet anything that holds such power over us—whether it be Baal or Hootie and the Blowfish—is already being worshipped. If art is feared more than God, then art is the object of our worship.

Either way, darkness wins. Whatever gooses our hearts into a wild turkey chase away from loving God and our neighbor extravagantly is the true tool of darkness. And whatever gives us more satisfaction than God—whether it's art, or the self-righteous, smug bashing of art, or even the time-consuming ambivalence of deciding what we *believe* about art—is a lurching, gruesome idol of stone, meant to turn our hearts into granite themselves. Counterfeits.

We were designed with an altogether different purpose in mind: To be the genuine article of artistry—people who create works that breathe humanity, works that reflect our God. A God who longs to turn battery-dead hearts of useless religion . . . into hearts of alive, ticking flesh. The real thing. Filled with the right stuff.

Thank God, art is not God.

But God *is* Art.

CREATIVE SPIRITUAL EXERCISE: *Journal this week about your spiritual tendencies as an artist. Do you ever turn to art instead of God? Or avoid art at times because it seems too dangerous? Try writing a psalm of praise, celebrating your freedom as an artist of the soul.*

33

PALM BRANCHES OF PARADOX

*An artist recreates those aspects
of reality which represent his fundamental
view of man's nature.*

—AYN RAND

*T*he writer Ayn Rand, best known for her novels *The Fountainhead* and *Atlas Shrugged*, was first and foremost a philosopher. Her philosophy, objectivism, combines politics, ethics, epistemology, and metaphysics, defining man's ability to reason as the highest power in the universe. According to Rand, man's sole purpose in life is the achievement of personal happiness. Objectivism rejects any form of determinism, including belief in God, on the grounds that, in order to be moral, man must live for himself.

In other words, I'll have my cake and eat it, too—and even hoard the crumbs.

The documentary film *Ayn Rand: A Sense of Life* tells the story of how Rand came to America from her homeland of Russia in the mid-1920s. As a teenager, she witnessed both the Kerensky and Bolshevik Revolutions, and her experience of these crises helped determine her life's direction. While studying philosophy and history at the University of Petrograd, Rand discovered a joyous escape from the drudgery of communist militancy: American films and plays. Soon, her goal became simple—to leave the USSR for good and to become a screenwriter. After obtaining permission to leave her country to visit American relatives on a short visit, she spent six months with some Chicago relatives, arranged for a visa extension—and then headed straight for Hollywood.

During her first interview, Rand was unable to land a job. But, while standing by the studio gate on her second day in Hollywood, a fortuitous event occurred: She was spotted by the director Cecil B. DeMille. He stopped her, asked about her life—and promptly suggested she ride with him to the set of his new movie. When Rand told him her dilemma, he then offered her a job—as an extra on the set of a new movie he was making. She accepted.

The movie was DeMille's *King of Kings*.

Ironically, the first job held by the future founder of objectivism was to wave palm branches in praise to Jesus as he rode by. Ayn Rand got her start in Hollywood—by paying enthusiastic homage to the very God she later rejected.

Paradox is a palpable fruit of the kingdom of God. That's because Jesus is the supreme master of irony. He turns things upside down, sideways, catty-corner—any way but what's expected. Looking for a monarch born in vibrant, velveteen splendor? *Not,* he says. I'm the God of nubby burlap and crude pine and fetid hay. Looking to worm your way into the coveted inner circle of the lifestyles of the rich and famous? Not if you're mine, he says. I've called you as my friends to AIDS patients and alcoholics and Albanian refugees. Looking to get a good investment by hoarding all your money somewhere? Nope. Give it, give it, give it, he says, as much as you can. Your broker lives in heaven.

As Ayn Rand says, "The artist recreates those aspects of reality which represent his fundamental view of man's nature." Indeed.

Artists of the soul take the poetry of kingdom paradox and bring it to life. Art—writing and painting and dancing—takes the ignored, little amoebas of this world and examines them under the microscope of broader vision. The paradox of art is the big "hah-hah" in this life—the fact that nothing is as it appears. Everything will one day be revealed. But for now, artists of the soul offer others a tiny sliver of God's upside-down cake. They dish out paradoxical slices of the kingdom.

In the midst of a world that is largely at home with Ayn Rand's man-centered philosophy of "I'll have my cake and eat it, too," the apostle Paul reminds us of what God's cooked up as his ultimate paradox: Someday, he says, every person on earth will fall on his or her knees—and proclaim that Jesus Christ is Lord (Rom. 14:11). Until then, we may have our cake—but it tastes better when we share it with as many people as possible.

One day, everyone will get a chance to wave palm branches of paradox—as Ayn Rand once did so fervently on the set of a movie classic. But this time, no one will be acting. DeMille's King of Kings will be riding through—for real.

SCRIPTURE MEDITATION: *Then I saw Heaven open wide—and oh! a white horse and its Rider. The Rider, named Faithful and True, judges and makes war in pure righteousness. His eyes are a blaze of fire, on his head many crowns. He has a Name inscribed that's known only to himself. He is dressed in a robe soaked with blood, and he is addressed as "Word of God." The armies of Heaven, mounted on white horses and dressed in dazzling white linen, follow him. . . . On his robe and thigh is written, KING OF KINGS, LORD OF LORDS* (Rev. 19:11–14, 16 *The Message*).

34

DRAGGING ONE ANOTHER THROUGH THE MUD

Even if my marriage is falling apart and
my children are unhappy there is still part of
me that says . . . This is fascinating!

—JANE SMILEY,
AUTHOR OF *A THOUSAND ACRES*

hen God created the world, he created *ex nihilo*—out of nothing. There was no time, no space, no little green men from Mars. It's not even fair to call the nothingness a blank canvas on which he painted, because there was no canvas. His act of creation—including creating us—set him apart forever as the most incredible Artist, Writer, Dancer, Playwright of the ages. He created a sun brighter than Van Gogh's sunflowers. The passionate poetry of planets and stars. He even went swing-dancing across the vast ballroom of the ocean floor. And, in the seventh act of the epic play, he rested—a reminder to us of the eternal delight there is in stopping to relax and contemplate the artistry of God.

Yet of all God's grand artistic projects, it seems he experienced the most joy in . . . making mudpies. God the Sculptor sat down and scooped a handful of earth, moistened and patted and shaped it, and formed it into man. Man, the magnificent mudpie. From the common, base elements of the ground, the Creator fashioned his most prized portrait in the gallery of the galaxy.

As human beings made in the image of God, we are all creators. We are all artisans. Yet we are something else as well: Like God, we are all mudpie makers. Created in the image of the Mudpie-Maker, we've inherited what I call "mudpie theology."

J. M. Thornburn said, "All the genuine, deep delight in life is in showing people the mudpies you have made; and life is at its best when we confidingly recommend our mudpies to each other's sympathetic consideration." That seems like good advice. No matter how old we are, or where we are at in the creative process, or what we are going through currently, the deepest delight comes in sharing our mudpies—the earthy substance of our lives—with one another.

Many writers and artists will tell you that the basis for the artistic process hinges on their fascination with the most common, base elements of their everyday lives (see Jane Smiley's quotation at the beginning of this meditation). Art leaps from arguments between husbands and wives, from kids who misbehave at Toys-R-Us.

For example, who would think one could stay riveted to the movie screen for the entire two hours of *My Dinner with Andre*—a film that consists entirely of Wallace Shawn and Andre Gregory talking over a meal? (I forget if the dessert was maybe . . . mud pie?) Or that Nicholson Baker's entire novel *The Mezzanine* consists of a brief ride up an escalator?

Mudpie theology splatters across our clean, white protests that we can't create because our lives are too boring. Wal-Mart shoppers, tabloid readers, mothers of toddlers, take notice: You are prime candidates when it comes to the artistic sensibilities of mudpie theology. God made his favorite creation, man, out of the most common elements of earth, dirt and water. So, whether you're looking for a cheap vacuum sweeper, learning the latest dirt on mail-order vitamins, or dusting for grubby handprints to find out which child *really* broke Grandma's favorite lamp, you're smack in the mudhole of where real art gets created. And, when you offer us your mudpies, you connect with us at the deepest level possible. Because all of us, whether we spend our days looking at Monet or Mickey Mouse, share common elements. We each create out of the earthen realities of our lives—mixed with the fresh water of the Spirit.

"We have this treasure in earthen vessels," Paul says, "so that the power others see might be of God, and not us" (2 Cor. 4:7). It's the very mud of human experience that allows us to squash and squish the material of our lives into art. And God's infusing that material allows others to see him as the ultimate Creator.

The prophet Zechariah said centuries before Paul, "Despise not the day of small things." The art of mudpie-making honors the day, the hour, the millisecond of small things—and offers it to others for their enjoyment. And everyone in the process (including you) is bound to have fun, because the mudpie playground has only one rule: the messier, the better.

Think of it this way: No one fails at making mudpies—except those who won't get dirty. So let's be faithful to drag one another . . . through the mud.

CREATIVE EXERCISE: *Make an artistic mudpie this week— something created from one of your life's more common elements—to give to someone else.*

35

Perspectives on Popeye

> *What is art but a way of seeing?*
> —THOMAS BERGER

*I*n his painting *The Suffering of Christ* (circa 1304–06), Giotto di Bondone vividly portrays the grief of Jesus' family and friends after his death. As weeping angels hover overhead, wringing their hands, Mary embraces her dead son for the last time.

Although the painting might appear typical for its time period, it actually represented a revolutionary new approach to art. During the fourteenth century, painters worked under a strict code of rules. The Old and New Testament characters who could be painted were already predetermined, as well as the structure of the painting itself, or what was called the "perspective of meaning." Through the lens of the perspective of meaning, the most important subjects in the painting appeared the largest, and the least important ones smallest. In addition, anything in the painting that represented God's order usually was tinged with gold.

Di Bondone made a radical departure from the norm in *The Suffering of Christ*. The picture had new depth—a clearly recognizable foreground and background, instead of the traditional, flat pictorial representation. The humans and angels pictured were no longer lifeless caricatures; they were living, breathing, feeling, grieving subjects. The "gold halo" effect was replaced with gritty realism. Nothing was seen as more or less important as anything else. Breathy, celestial faith was fused with the solid, raw earth. And a new art form was born—because the artist dared to see his subjects three-dimensionally.

Christ saw three-dimensionally too. Instead of caricaturing all Pharisees as "white-washed tombs," we also see him singling out the spiritually-hungry Nicodemus, a religious bigwig in the Jewish ruling council. And in the course of Christ's conversation with the right-wing Nicodemus, we're given some of the most quoted words in the entire Bible: "For God so loved the world that he gave his one and only Son, that whoever believes in him shall not perish but have eternal life" (John 3:16 NIV). Those were words coming from an entirely different perspective—a radical departure from the current Law. And they were spoken to one who was already lumped into a group of people clearly on the "outs" with Jesus.

What about Christ's anything-but-flat response to that straight-shooter, Nathanael? When Philip tells Nathanael that he's got to meet this new guy, Jesus, from Nazareth, Nathanael laughs in his face. "How in the world can anything good come out of *Nazareth*?" he hoots. Yet when Jesus shakes Nat's hand upon meeting him, he chortles happily, "Here's a true Israelite, in whom there is no guile!" Nathanael, surprised, responds, "How in the world do you know what kind of guy I am?" Jesus answers him and says, "I saw you when you were sitting under a fig tree, before Philip came and got you and brought you to me" (see John 1:43–50).

Christ saw something out of the immediate range of sight, something beyond what was most obvious in the person-painting in front of him. He saw something no one else saw—an Israelite who could tell the unadulterated truth. An exception to the rule. He didn't penalize Nathanael for laughing at the absurdity of his having come from a dump called Nazareth. Again, for Jesus, there were no caricatures, no cartoons—only people. No Popeyes, only Picassos.

Unlike Jesus, we can't supernaturally see Nathanael sitting under a fig tree down the road. But, through his love, we can see the Nathanaels and the Nicodemuses in our lives three-dimensionally. We can refuse to caricature, to pigeonhole, to stereotype, to give in to the dull, uncreative pull of prejudice. We can choose to see people as the artist Giotti di Bondone painted them—so real that we taste their tears, whoop it up at their birthday parties, laugh at their sarcastic jokes about our birthplaces.

That three-dimensional thinker, the apostle Paul, had good words for this artistic venture: "So from now on we regard no one from a worldly point of view" (2 Cor. 5:16 NIV). Meaning, we don't look at anybody the same way we did before knowing God's love. Through Christ's creative lens, we can see what others either refuse to see or are afraid to see because it cuts against the political correctness of the culture. We can broaden our canvases, enlarge our tent pegs. We can risk painting more than comfortable, one-dimensional cartoons of vision and love. We can gain new perspectives on Popeye.

PRAYER: *God, allow me to see the people in my life three-dimensionally. Open my eyes to your endless creativity alive in those around me, and show me how to lovingly encourage diversity.*

36

Swimming in Spirituality's Sea of Poetry

> *The poet—when he is writing—is a priest;*
> *the poem is a temple; epiphanies and communion*
> *take place within it.*
>
> —DENISE LEVERTOV

*I*n Acts 17, when the apostle Paul visits the city of Athens, he sweats through a strenuous cultural—and spiritual—workout. The town is full of Epicurean and Stoic philosophers who like to shoot the breeze on virtually every wind of intellectual discourse. (The same people today would hang out at the local Starbucks, sipping lattes and arguing over the validity of deconstructionism and postmodernism.) Yet the Apostle's relentless, persuasive patter on the simple power of the resurrection so fascinates these deep thinkers, they invite him to make a public speech on the topic. Paul seizes the media opportunity by utilizing the Athenians' own philosophy, poetry, religion, and basic logic in order to lead them to a rudimentary knowledge of God.

He begins his resurrection talk at the renowned Areopagus by honoring how incredibly religious these people are—highlighting the fact that he'd even enjoyed stumbling across an altar inscribed TO THE UNKNOWN GOD. You guys truly *are* seekers, Paul says. However, you don't have to worship something unknown anymore. The God you're searching for is the God of heaven and earth—a God who doesn't live in temples: "The God who made the world and everything in it, this Master of sky and land, doesn't live in custom-made shrines or need the human race to run errands for him, as if he couldn't take care of himself . . . One of your poets said it well: 'We're the God-created.' Well, if we are God-created, it doesn't make a lot of sense to think we could hire a sculptor to chisel a god out of stone for *us*, does it?" (see *The Message*, vv. 24–25 28–29).

Paul pulls out all the academic and pop culture he knows, in order to meet the Athenians on common ground. But first he treats their religious folklore respectfully—in order to present the risen Lord.

Like the intellects Paul encountered in Athens, artists today are often incredibly spiritual people. And when you plunge whole-heartedly into the colorful swimming pool of poetry or photography or painting, more than likely you'll tread water next to people who wear every kind of religious flotation device imaginable. Tread lightly, though: You might want to temporarily shelve your five-pound book of apologetics. The Areopagus is no arena for arid answers, so cool down. America is swimming with sunglazed spirituality—and, like Paul, you may want to share your faith "the artist's way." Put on your sunglasses and travel incognito.

The artist-of-the-soul's way is to immerse yourself in a craft—or a culture—so thoroughly that, just as the Apostle did, you connect Chekhov and Christ, Chagall and Christ, Kant and Christ (or maybe even the Chicago White Sox and Christ). There is a thin thread that separates art from religion. A thin thread separates *spirituality* from *Christ*. Spiritually hungry artists often lurk so close to truth's edge that your art-connected nudge can cause a (surprise!) belly-flop straight into Jesus' vast pool of purposeful beauty. The same holds true for various religions: Your careful understanding and respectful navigation of Deepak Chopra's beliefs could lead a friend or fellow artist to deeper universal undercurrents.

In Acts 17, the poet-priest Paul's words end up making quite a spiritual splash. He attaches a short line of verse to a fishing hook for the Gospel, and his speech tugs at us for all time. The poet of the soul is the artist who baits—and waits—patiently on the bridge between Christ and culture, between Poetry and religion.

POETRY AND RELIGION

Religions are poems. The concert
our daylight and dreaming mind, our
emotions, instinct, breath and native gesture

into the while thinking: poetry.
Nothing's said till it's dreamed out in words
and nothing's true that figures in words only.

A poem, compared with an arrayed religion,
may be like a soldier's one short marriage night
to die and live by. But that is a small religion.

Full religion is the large poem flowing in repetition;
like any poem, it must be inexhaustible and complete
with turns where we ask *Now why did the poet do that?*

You can't pray a lie, said Huckleberry Finn;
you can't poe one either. It is the same mirror:
mobile, glancing, we call it poetry,

fixed centrally, we call it a religion,
and God is the poetry caught in any religion,

caught, not imprisoned. Caught as in a mirror
that he attracted, being in the world as poetry
is in the poem, a law against its closure.
There'll always be religion around while there is poetry

or a lack of it. Both are given, and intermittent,
as the action of those birds—crested pigeon, rosella parrot—
who fly with wings shut, then beating, then again shut.

—LES MURRAY

SCRIPTURE MEDITATION: *From one man he made every nation of men, that they should inhabit the whole earth; and he determined the times set for them and the exact places where they should live. God did this so that men would seek him and perhaps reach out for him and find him, though he is not far from each one of us. "For in him we live and move and have our being." As some of your own poets have said, "We are his offspring"* (Acts 17:26–28 NIV).

37

DEAD MEN'S CURVE

*Show me the books he loves and
I shall know the man far better than
through mortal friends.*

—DAWN ADAMS

The art of mentoring is a frequently discussed topic these days. And with good reason: Artists, as well as artists of the soul, are thirsty to locate others they can learn from, ask questions of, imitate. Yet the fast-paced culture we travel in, as well as geographical obstacles, frequently challenge us in fulfilling this longing.

Some people say the contemplative life is the answer. Just slow down your lifestyle, they say. Get rid of your daytimer. Slowliness is next to godliness. (Might work for some. Like John, on the Isle of Patmos. But this hardly fits the bill for God's highly-scheduled itinerary for Paul, that anything-but-stay-at-home-and-sip-lemonade kind of guy.)

Others believe the Internet can solve our cultural problem. So you're a beginning portrait painter in Whoiswarhol, Iowa? A burgeoning evangelist in Iwannabefinney, Michigan? Through the miracle of e-mail, you can now study with the artist or seminary professor of your choice. There's plenty of room to chat . . . about Warhol *or* Finney.

Actually, in any given situation, a more contemplative lifestyle—one that allows you time with a mentor, and he/she with you—or an Internet extension course or correspondence course, could be just what the soul-doctor orders. The opportunity to learn from or study with others in the winter of their journey can be one of the most nourishing seasons of the soul.

But if you find yourself currently "mentor challenged," it might be encouraging to recall a couple of simple biblical truths:

Our circumstantial lack doesn't affect our calling.

And our best mentors are often dead guys.

Paul tells us this himself: Whether he was rich, poor, verbally assaulted, praised, depressed, overjoyed, criticized, lauded—mentored or unmentored—this artist of the soul kept right on going, creating his powerful epistles of faith and hope, trusting in the power of Christ within to sustain him (1 Cor. 4). He knew a wonderful secret: That the resurrection life of Jesus cannot be entombed by anything external. And, not only that, but Paul himself was mentorless: He started preaching, sans human discipler, within days of becoming a Christian (see Acts 9:20). (Artists—take encouragement. You don't always need a class from the Parsons School of Design to know what you're doing.)

There's something else, though: Notice whom Paul mentions as his heroes. Not anyone he's actually sat down with over a hot cappucino. They're all the faithful players in the Cooperstown Hall of Christianity, God's all-stars listed in Hebrews 11. Paul, the spiritually hard-hitting pro in the faith, bats around the names of dead guys.

We're never without a great cloud of mentors. There is an abundance to be cherished—not only among Paul's litany, but through the art of *lectio divina,* spiritual reading. For soul-challenge, encouragement, and comfort, there are men and women whose lives and words speak to us across time and culture: St. John of the

Cross, Bernard of Clairvaux, Fenelon, St. Teresa of Avila, Thomas à Kempis, John Bunyan, William Law, John Wesley.

As artists, we can probably name those creative people we've read about, whose work has set the curve, raised the standard for us. Yet, often, it's not necessarily they, but their *art,* that has mentored us.

Sometimes, it's hard to swallow that our hunger is a good thing: "Blessed are those who hunger and thirst," Jesus says in Matthew 5, "for they shall be filled." Sometimes it is our deepest longings that propel us to forge new artistic ground. Sometimes it's what we haven't tasted that teaches us how and what to feed others. And sometimes it is in the act of forgetting ourselves and nourishing others . . . that we discover we've somehow already been mysteriously fed.

Paul's life and talk of dead men throws us a cultural curve ball: He simply saw himself as a disciple of Christ. And others were taught—mentored—because he was, first and foremost, a follower of Jesus. It was through the *result* of Paul following Christ—*God's creative art formed within him*—that others read his words . . . and grew.

If you put the Art first, it will lead you. And, in the art of the soul, the living Art is the one who sets the curve.

SCRIPTURE MEDITATION: *I've learned by now to be quite content whatever my circumstances. I'm just as happy with little as with much, with much as with little. I've found the recipe for being happy whether full or hungry, hands full or hands empty. Whatever I have, wherever I am, I can make it through anything in the One who makes me who I am* (Phil. 4:11–13 *The Message*).

38

Baby Steps

All real art comes from the deepest self—
painting, writing music, and dance, all of it that in
some way nourishes the spirit and
enriches the understanding.

—FREDERICK BUECHNER

*J*n her enlightening essay "To Fashion a Text," Annie Dillard offers her view of writing:

"Writing a book is like rearing children—willpower has very little to do with it. If you have a little baby crying in the middle of the night, and if you depend only on willpower to get you out of bed to feed the baby, that baby will starve. You do it out of love. Willpower is a weak idea; love is strong. You don't have to scourge yourself with a cat-o'-nine-tails to go to the baby. You go to the baby out of love for that particular baby. That's the same way you go to your desk. There's nothing freakish about it. Caring passionately about something isn't against nature, and it isn't against human nature. It's what we're here to do."

Creating, Dillard says, is not an esoteric, self-flagellating act of duty. It is as natural as wanting to love and care for our children. The Latin word for *creator* means, literally, to "make offspring." God gave birth to us, and we in turn give birth to others—and to our books and plays and films and operas and folk songs and crocheting and gardens. Our creations are like helpless, mewing infants that we gently nurture, cuddle and change as they stretch and grow into maturity. Like tiptoeing into a baby's room to peek into his crib, it is love—sheer love, pure, unadorned love—that will motivate us to return to our creations, again and again. As Dillard notes, willpower is a weak idea. Our art—like our deepest selves—is not developed simply by duty, but by desire. Love is *strong*.

Perhaps you're familiar with the words of 1 Corinthians 13, where Paul patiently explains the hallmarks of genuine love. This is one of the most humbling passages in the Bible, because it makes us realize we are all dependent upon the Spirit's feeding and nurturing in order to grow into maturity. It is also an especially humbling passage for artists. A ballpark paraphrase of the first few verses might read: "If I can write with the voice of Elizabeth Barrett Browning, but I don't have love, I am only a resounding gong or a clanging cymbal. If I have the gift of creating piercing prophetic lyrics like Bruce Cockburn's or can fathom the mysteries of Marcel or the knowledge of Kierkegaard, and if I have the faith to create a revolutionary approach to copper sculpture, but I have not love, I am nothing. If I give all my royalties to Habitat for Humanity, or even give up all my art to become a missionary to Bosnia and die for my faith, but I have not love, I gain nothing" (vv. 1–3).

How does God's love develop within our hearts? How do we grow the love that "believes all things, hopes all things, endures all things"? The answer is as basic as Annie Dillard's relationship to her writing. Willpower doesn't have a whole lot to do with the process.

It goes without saying that God the Creator approaches his creative process in us just as Dillard describes approaching her writing desk. He does it with desire. He doesn't simply grit his teeth and endure us. No, he *loves* his art. Imagine him, peeking over the crib-edge of the sky, looking down at us, his creations—his squalling and blubbering and pooping babies. And yet, his look is one of delight, of pleasure. Of love.

"We love," says the apostle John, "because he first loved us" (1 John 4:19 NIV). If we want to be loving artists of the soul—those who approach God, others, and our art with love—we can start by allowing ourselves *to be loved.* We can soak our soul's fingertips in the spiritual dishwashing liquid that purifies everything it touches: God's love.

The beginning point of all creating, of all spiritual life, isn't our love; it is *his.* "This is love," John says, "Not that we loved God, but that he loved us and sent his Son as an atoning sacrifice for our sins" (4:10). As Annie Dillard might say, caring passionately isn't something against either nature or human nature. It is what we are here to do. It is a reflection of the Creator's passion—the love he showed us in sending an infant for our redemption.

His love first stepped toward us as a baby. And our baby steps in response are simply to allow ourselves to believe in that awesome love. That's how we first learn to love him—and others—in return. If we depend solely on willpower to create, or to love, we'll starve the Baby cradled in our souls. It is the power of his love that can wake up our heart—and our art—in the dead of this world's night.

SCRIPTURE MEDITATION: *If anyone acknowledges that Jesus is the Son of God, God lives in him and he in God. And so we know and **rely** on the love God has for us. God is love. Whoever lives in love lives in God, and God in him* (1 John 4:15–16 NIV, emphasis added).

39

ACTING OUT OF INSECURITY

*Insecurity, commonly regarded
as weakness in normal people, is the
basic tool of the actor's trade.*

—MIRANDA RICHARDSON

Let's just get the truth right out on the coffee table, shall we? We human beings struggle with insecurity. It often lurks beneath whatever glossy package we're wrapped in—whether it's the size of our thighs, our thinning hairline, or our faulty opinions on theology or thespian performances. (I add this last one, since my husband and I are currently struggling deeply with "thespian insecurity." Three years in a row, our good friends Dave and Shari Meserve have trumped us with their picks at our annual guess-the-winner Oscar get-together. And my husband is a film critic. Shari would like all of you to know this.) Yet, as actress Miranda Richardson says above, insecurity doesn't have to be a liability for the good actor. It can be his or her greatest strength—if used well. It can provide the molten creative fuel that energizes a performance.

For those of us who pursue God's art of the heart, we often encounter paradoxical stage directions in our soul. One of these centers on the issue of weakness. In God's kingdom, just like in a good actor's work, the very thing that would ordinarily be labeled a great liability is turned into creative fodder for the journey. We don't know what the apostle Paul's particular weakness was, but we do know that Miranda Richardson's words echo his perspective. He tells us that something in his life brought him to the end of his resources and down to his knees. After asking God to remove what he calls "a thorn in the flesh," Paul receives a most countercultural answer from the Lord of paradox: "My grace is sufficient for you, for power is perfected in weakness," God tells him. Paul moves on from describing that encounter to say that he gladly boasts about his weaknesses, that the power of Christ can rest on him—can build his Spirit's stage set in his heart (2 Cor. 12:8–9 NASB).

When we embrace the truth about insecurity or weakness, we can stumble into freedom's enormous spotlight. And suddenly, the very things in our lives that pull down the curtains of shame on our souls can also raise the curtains of God's grace. Even if others may not know what our particular thorn is, like Paul we can be channels of the paradox of power: God is pleased to work through people who need him desperately. And others can and will witness and experience that power in our lives, as we seek to glory in Christ.

Many who sign up to participate in God's unfolding drama somehow find themselves stuck between the first and second acts of the play. The first? We come to him in our utter need for him and are forgiven. Accepted. Loved. Transformed. And then given a prime, juicy role—since every role in the body of Christ is just as needed as the next.

The second act of the play, however—living the life of faith—requires listening to the script of the kingdom, not the script of the world. And in that divine script, God wants to work through us, not through our own power but through his. We may have one talent, ten talents, or a hundred—but the spiritual stage we act on requires dependence on the Spirit's stage management to guide us through our moves.

The way of the world will loudly shout its own directions: *The only people of use are the strong ones, the together ones, the ones who are secure and stable.* And sometimes, we can be fooled into thinking those qualities are what we see in people, when really we're glimpsing the Spirit's work through them. The apostle Paul looks pretty polished in most every letter he writes (he's a good writer, after all). It's only by reading *all* his words that we know the secret to his life's work: he desperately needed God to show up in each and every scene of his "second act." We can take courage from his example of dependence.

When this life's finale arrives someday, no doubt we'll hold hands in the solidarity of gratitude. We'll bow to the One who magnificently directed us with such joy and mercy, such strength and beauty, such incredible creativity. We'll be made whole, perfect. Without weakness, without thorns, forever.

Yet until then, we can simply "act out of insecurity"—and let God direct our lives as actors and agents of his power in the world.

CREATIVE SPIRITUAL EXERCISE: *What are some of your weaknesses? Journal and pray this week about the creative things God may want to do through your dependence on him.*

40

CHRIST, OUR VANISHING POINT

Art, that great undogmatized church.

—ELLEN KEY

*T*he fifteenth-century artist Masaccio startled the church-going sensibilities of his time. In his groundbreaking painting *The Holy Trinity* (circa 1427), he used a spatial illusion to create a tableau of the Father, Son, and Holy Ghost. The painting appeared so visually "real" that Masaccio's first viewers thought he'd knocked down a wall to reveal an adjoining chapel. His artistic finesse is displayed in a work where God and man were on the same visual plane—creating the effect that we are actually in the same room where the Trinity communes.

Masaccio's work, like Giotto di Bondone, was pioneering in his time by directly connecting both the common and the sacred life. Up to that point in time, much of the character of Christ's humanity had been obscured, and Renaissance artists such as Masaccio and Bondone visually brought back a much-needed earthiness to church life.

Yet the "realness" of *The Holy Trinity* actually derived from an artistic perspective implemented earlier by the sculptor and architect Filippo Brunelleschi. He believed that everything in a painting must head toward one single point, called the *vanishing point*. This *vanishing point* creates the startling view that Masaccio employed so beautifully in his painting.

In the art of the soul, Christ is the vanishing point toward which everything heads. Like Masaccio's painting, he holds together the truth-tension of transcendence and reality in one place. He is the place of renaissance, the place where both human and divine lines meet, where all things converge: "And He is the image of the invisible God, the first-born of all creation. For by Him all things were created, both in the heavens and on earth, visible and invisible, whether thrones or dominions or rulers or authorities—all things have been created by Him and for Him. And He is before all things, and in Him all things hold together" (Col. 1:15–18 NASB).

Christ is the place where all aspects of God connect in complete and perfect equilibrium. This image can help us immensely, since sometimes our images of God can be painted too heavily in one direction or the other. For instance, somewhere in our soul's grandstands we might have encountered God as an austere, removed, angry Coach—a grouchy Law-giver who tosses lightning bolts like javelins when we don't perform well on the running track of life. Or we might have adopted a teddy-bear, buddy-God whom we haul around like a good-luck charm—a vapid, pink, fluffy God who exists only to fuzzinate our lives with sweetness and bliss. Or any number of other God-versions.

That's why Christ came. He is the awesome God in awful flesh; He is the worthy-of-worship One who washed our feet. We can look at Christ, the perfect painting of God, and see the image of him who "holds all things together"—the image of both the human and divine. When our image of God is too "crusty" (as a friend of mine likes to say), Jesus whispers kindly, "Remember? I've called you friends." When our image is too "buddy-buddy," Jesus offers the puzzling reminder that "the road is narrow; no one gets to the Father except through me."

Like Massacio's art, Christ our Vanishing Point gives us a breathtaking view into the splendor of the Father, Son, and Holy Ghost. When we look at him, it is as if the wall of illusion or misdirected belief that stands between us and God is removed—and, like a Renaissance painting, we can suddenly see the real, the holy. The human, the divine. Gilded curves of grace and the straight lines of the law.

All in one glimpse of beauty.

PRAYER:

Late have I loved you, O Beauty so ancient and so new; late have I loved you! . . . You called me and cried to me and broke upon my deafness; you sent forth your beams and shone upon me and chased away my blindness; you breathed your fragrance upon me, and I drew in my breath and now I pant for you; I tasted you, and now I hunger and thirst for you; you touched me, and I burn for your peace.

—ST. AUGUSTINE OF HIPPO

41

METAPHORICALLY SPEAKING . . .

A novel is never anything
but a philosophy put into images.

—ALBERT CAMUS

*O*ver the years, the novelist Larry Woiwode has created a distinctive, incarnational body of work: *Poppa John, Indian Affairs, Beyond the Bedroom Wall, Born Brothers*—novels that powerfully engage our senses through our connection with their very human, affecting characters. Woiwode, a Christian who embraces reformed theology, is also known to stir in more than a spoonful of faith into his plots: "*Beyond the Bedroom Wall* is a Christian novel of the covenant," he says, "of four generations of a family resting on God's grace or rebelling against it."

Woiwode is also a profoundly soul-provoking biblical essayist. In a recent *Books & Culture* article, "The Word Made Flesh," Woiwode discusses the power of the metaphor—and The Metaphor. He directly connects our ability to write poetically, or to create convincing fictional characters, with the nature of our faith: "Metaphor makes words flesh. Metaphor opens our eyes to applying The Word. So metaphor makes the world of The Word fresh . . . .

"I believe there never would have risen from humankind the idea that flesh-and-blood characters could be fashioned from words if The Word hadn't come in the flesh. Jesus.

"This holds for all the arts when they assume a metaphorical substance that communicates some attribute of God. The reality of this is always more exciting than any theory, when we hold or stand in front of such a work, or hear its music run through us and realize, *This is it.*"

The metaphor of the word—it's an endless metaphor if you are a writer or artist steeped in the beauty of The Word. Yet there are so many metaphors to explore, to create from—including the faith-images indelibly impressed upon our souls: light, salt, shepherd, eagle, wind, breath, refuge, healer, fire, warrior, gardener, farmer, potter. As we meditate upon the metaphors of our God, the art of the soul is stirred, awakened—we want to know more of his texture, color, aroma.

We communicate a spiritual reality through our art when we have tasted, touched, handled the Metaphor for ourselves. Such art has soaked in truth and spirit, and cannot help but radiate the presence, the power, the spirit of the ineffable Other.

A friend told me he was once driving on the freeway in his car listening to a classical radio station. Suddenly he heard for the first time the Polish Catholic composer Henryk Gorecki's *Third Symphony (Symphony of Sorrowful Songs)*. The music affected him so profoundly that he broke down crying. He drove to a pay phone after the song's end and called the radio station to find out what the title of the piece was. Gorecki's symphony is music permeated with the metaphor of the healer, offering the hope of faith even while expressing tragedy's sting. As Larry Woiwode says of metaphor, its music ran through my friend until he said, *This is it.*

The Word made flesh implies both humility and power. It implies One who came as one of us—but one who also came, and comes, as The Word. Even though our art may not expound on the Scriptures, its very nature contains The Word, Christ's presence.

And his presence always affects—moves, changes, disturbs, comforts—just as each of the biblical metaphors do in their contexts. Metaphors are the gate-crashers of the spiritually *static* quo.

When Paul writes to the Thessalonian believers, he reflects on the manner in which the gospel came to them: ". . . not simply with words, but also with power, with the Holy Spirit and with deep conviction" (1 Thess. 1:5 NIV). This was also noted of Jesus when he delivered his message—that he spoke as one having authority, not as the scribes. Not a power-wielding, oppressive authority—but the quiet confidence, the comforting presence, the convicting voice of The Metaphor. The scribes' dull rhetoric was mere persuasive words; The Metaphor's living art is the power to open blind eyes.

For every artist of the soul, may the splendor of The Metaphor communicate beyond the power of our own human creations.

CREATIVE EXERCISE: *Choose a biblical metaphor—one you've never used before—and create a work of art this week.*

42

REAPING THE CROSS-POLLINATED, CREATIVE HARVEST

Paul Valery speaks on
the "une ligne donnee" of a poem.
One line is given to the poet by God or by nature,
the rest he has to discover for himself.

—STEPHEN SPENDER

My writing mentor once admitted to me that he hates to write. But he loves *having written*. The actual process of starting to write, he says, is best summed up by the pedantic, very unromantic, "Apply rear to chair." It's true: Writing is work—hard, taxing work. But it is also glorious work, similar to the way a gardener feels when his tomatoes bud and ripen on the vine. Writing is movement. Writing is life.

Some poets talk about the incredible experience of having an entire poem "given" to them. "It was like taking dictation," says one. "I merely took the words down as fast as I could write them, and there were nearly no revisions. It felt holy."

Those are rare, sacred moments, meant to be enjoyed. Yet it's just as holy to persist in working on the poem or song or novel or scrapbook one has labored over for a decade or so. Perseverance, endurance, fortitude—these are the marks of the farmer and the artist. The farmer knows that the seed he planted in the exuberant springtime is taking root through the bitter, bleak winter. Likewise, artists know that, even while they're hoeing and tilling the hard soil of stagnation, there's something utterly redemptive in the whole process.

In fact, sometimes it's the process itself—not the finished product—that becomes the actual harvest. Often in the labor of endurance we discover what we're made of and what we're in need of. To not grow weary in creative well-doing is to know that true fruitfulness is found not in success but in struggle. Faithfulness is what cultivates the creative soil needed to produce the crop—a harvest that smells strangely like the glorious, ripe grain of glory.

To say that the process of creating is just plain, hard work is true. But it's work that makes our heart pump wildly with life, causing the blood of purpose to course through our finite, earth-bound veins. It is work that is good, good for the soul, a physical elixir to counteract spiritual fatigue and lethargy. In fact, the work of creating is the perfect parallel—and picture—of life with God.

When I am about to begin the creative process, then quickly give in to the "urgent" need to call my good friend in Nashville (the one I could call on Saturday and have a much longer conversation with), or to repaint my toenails fuschia instead of red (or should I choose peach?), I've directly encountered the dirt in my soul. I've unearthed that same rocky place that is capable of feeding a dark grudge, or making myself look good at someone else's expense. I'm soon lost in a swirling tornado of twisted, petty concerns, unable to discern what's most important. Digging hard soil—like forgiving, like loving, sometimes like creating—feels so unimportant at times, when instead it is the very act of life.

The process of planting is very plain; but the process of growing seed is nothing short of divine. This is the glory of the artist as disciple: When we do reap (and it will quite possibly be in the life to come, not here), we'll delight to see how creatively cross-pollinated our crop is. We'll see huge pumpkins, shiny eggplants, smooth-skinned cucumbers, things we ourselves never planted—but that came from our creative seeds, our soil.

Someday we will finally glimpse the harvest of unconscious kindnesses, long-forgotten acts of forgiveness, ordinary words of encouragement. The unheralded ordinary will be transformed into the shimmering grain of the stuff of glory. Our garden will be much more lush and wonderful and fun than we ever imagined, because we decided, in the ordinary moments of life and art, to put our hand to the plow of the simple, the hard, the rugged—and to never look back.

SCRIPTURE MEDITATION: *So let's not allow ourselves to get fatigued doing good. At the right time we will harvest a good crop if we don't give up, or quit. Right now, therefore, every time we get the chance, let us work for the benefit of all, starting with the people closest to us in the community of faith* (Gal. 6:9–10 *The Message*).

43

A Detailed,
Itemized Statement

The artist's vocation is to
send light into the human heart.

—ROBERT SCHUMANN

acKenzie-Childs is a vivid, distinctive style in the field of interior design and home furnishings. Artists Victoria and Richard MacKenzie-Childs produce hand-painted furniture, lamps, mouth-blown glassware, ceramic tiles, majolica dinnerware, linens, tassels, paper plates, and napkins—all created with their trademark flair. As one design writer describes their work, "MacKenzie-Childs home furnishings are a confluence of stripes and checks and plaids and florals and swirls and squiggles and dashes and dots and birds and bunnies and freckled fish—sometimes all on the same item."

The husband-and-wife team say their main artistic influence came through the years they spent working in England for the Lotus Pottery Company. As Victoria says, the villagers in the small town where they lived didn't know much about formal interior design. Their fireplace mantels were crammed with knick-knacks: ancestral portraits, vases, Christmas cards. Over time, the two artists fell in love with this "accidental" form of decorating.

But Victoria doesn't call their distinctive color-splashes and patterns "hodge-podge," as many might. "It's not a free-for-all," she says. "It's highly disciplined in a playful, confident way." Their product designs appear wild and untamed, but, on the contrary, they require the utmost artistic focus and restraint. In fact, they actually reflect the uninhibited use of formal structure.

According to Jesus, the kingdom of God has a paradoxical "interior design," much the way McKenzie-Childs creations do. This kingdom design liberates, even while requiring spiritual restraint. It both requires nothing and yet requires everything. It is uninhibited-yet-formal structure.

"Don't suppose for a minute that I have come to demolish the Scriptures—either God's Law or the Prophets," Jesus says. "I'm not here to demolish but to complete. I am going to put it all together, pull it all together in a vast panorama. God's Law is more real and lasting than the stars in the sky and the ground at your feet. Long after stars burn out and earth wears out, God's Law will be alive and working.

"Trivialize even the smallest item in God's Law and you will only have trivialized yourself. But take it seriously, show the way for others, and you will find honor in the kingdom" (Matt. 5:17–19 *The Message*).

Disrupting the artistic conventionality of those around him, Jesus explains in carefully hand-painted detail just how he takes the Law to its next creative level: "You know the next commandment pretty well, too. 'Don't go to bed with another's spouse.' But don't think you've preserved your virtue simply by staying out of bed. Your *heart* can be corrupted by lust even quicker than your *body*. Those leering looks you think nobody notices—they also corrupt" (5:27–28 *The Message*).

Christ himself is the one who pulls together all the artistic elements into one place. He gathers the stripes, checks, plaids, florals of the Law into one piece of freely-given Art: himself. When I paint my bright image on your heart, Jesus says, it won't be without design and structure. In fact, to create the pattern of my kingdom within your interior castle, I'm going to call you to live the commandments' colorful dots and squiggles in ways you've never even *thought* about combining them before.

In other words, Jesus says, I have a fine eye for detail. And I want you to, too. *Voilà.*

Psychologists say that children whose parents provide a good sense of formal structure in their lives often prove to be the most playful and carefree. Knowing the boundaries, these kids seem to possess more confidence to explore, to create. Our art—and the art of the soul—is the same way. Like a MacKenzie-Childs art piece, we have both the luxury and imposition of a highly intricate design on our souls. And we enjoy a greater sense of playfulness when we yield to the beauty of God's use of that structure in his human works of art.

Colorful, confetti freedom and red-plaid, disciplined order. The combination makes for some really wild and fun-looking stuff, you know? Pretty hard to ignore, too.

It's art that makes a statement. A detailed, itemized statement.

SCRIPTURE MEDITATION: *You're here to be light, bringing out the God-colors in the world. God is not a secret to be kept. We're going public with this, as public as a city on a hill. If I make you light-bearers, you don't think I'm going to hide you under a bucket, do you? I'm putting you on a light stand. Now that I've put you there on a hilltop, on a light stand—shine!* (Matt. 5:14–15 *The Message*).

44

WHY THE WHO IS ONTO WHAT'S FIRST

Music is the soul of art.

—JAMES BALDWIN BROWN

An acquaintance, whom I'll call Rick, tells this story: A few years ago, his sister, Lisa, was dying of a rare form of cancer. Seeing the harrowing struggle his sister faced from day to day, Rick constantly searched for everyday things he thought would make her happy. Lisa had always loved the music of The Who, and one day Rick noticed that band member Pete Townshend would be signing his newly-released book at a local bookstore. Rick made sure he arrived early to get an autographed copy. Still, the line of people ahead of him was already so long it wrapped around the entire block.

Several hours later, Rick finally approached the book table. He saw Townshend with his head lowered, furiously scribbling out signature after signature and shoving each book aside. When Rick reached the table, he haltingly explained to the singer who the book was for and why. Townshend never looked up. He just kept writing. Rick felt embarrassed, even a little angry. He kicked himself for even allowing himself to think he'd be treated any differently from anyone else in the crowded room.

When Rick reached the end of the swiftly moving assembly line, he picked up his book and looked inside—simply curious to see what the rock star's handwriting looked like. Yet instead of seeing a plain signature, Rich read this message: "To Lisa—Rise up and be healed! Pete Townshend." The singer had been listening after all. Very closely, in fact.

Ironically, Lisa eventually overcame her battle with cancer. She was, as Pete Townshend had written so hopefully, completely healed. The health she now enjoyed was made sweeter, Rich said, by the simple fact that, in the midst of a hectic day, a favorite musician had paid attention to the details of her life. Contrary to all appearances, Pete Townshend had indeed heard—and then written something special. Just for her.

The poet and novelist James Dickey defined a poet as "someone who notices and is enormously taken by things that somebody else would walk by." A main component of the poet's work is to highlight a common, ordinary detail so that we might see it through new eyes, hear it through new ears. Thus, the poet's senses are at work at all times, absorbing shades of periwinkle, nuances of marble shine, fragrances of juniper and jasmine, tender glances across a living room. Poetry, says yet another writer, is not a way of *saying* things but of *seeing* things. The poet's central vocation is not the writing of words themselves, but both possessing and nurturing the kind of vision and hearing that leads to the creation of those words.

In other words, the condition of your heart is what permeates your art.

The poet Jesus taught this very same artistic concept. Once some Pharisees complained to him about his disciples' behavior, grumbling that they neglected to wash their hands before eating—a spiritual taboo at the time. Jesus' followers weren't writing the words of the Scriptures accurately through their lives, the Pharisees accused.

Yet Jesus surprises these legalists by pinpointing an even finer poetic detail. He says it isn't what goes into a man's mouth that makes him unclean—not at all—but rather what comes out of his mouth. It is from deep within the heart, Jesus says, that soul-scabs fester and finally erupt, oozing murder, adultery, sexual immorality, theft, false testimony and slander (Matt. 15:11, 18–20). You people miss the important creative details, Jesus says. Poetry begins from within, not without. In other words, the Pharisees *knew the words but not the music.*

Some artists draw a sharp, definitive line between the sacred and the secular, between what is called "the world" and what is called "Christian." But such a stance is just another way of saying it's only what we absorb around us that makes us unclean. That our hearts are not the real source of our impure actions; society is. In practical terms, what is often labeled "Christian art" is not a way of seeing the world through God's eyes, but a way of saying things as drippingly religious as possible. Washing our hands of cultural grime as opposed to washing our souls of stubborn sin.

"To the pure," the apostle Paul says, "all things are pure" (Titus 1:15 NIV). But to those who allow the shadows of darkness to continue dancing secretly in the chambers of their souls, everything is impure, unclean. Historically, throughout the ages, some of the greatest demonstrations of truly worldly thinking—lust for money, power, sex—have cloaked themselves in heavy-duty religious garb. Think about it: The seductive lure of using the church's money to maintain a certain lifestyle (as opposed to steadfast faithfulness whether rich or poor). The compulsion to dominate rather than the simple desire to serve (whether behind the scenes or in the spotlight). And sex? Say no more.

In our assembly-line culture, a rock artist like Pete Townshend teaches us a lot about what our calling as soul-artists looks like. The real crux of the matter isn't the externals. It's possessing a poetic heart that affects our art—one that pays careful attention to Christ's details. It's having ears to hear what the Spirit is truly saying, so that, like Pete Townshend, we can write the hopeful, personalized words of God to those who are dying.

It's to know a Word steeped in plenty of music.

SCRIPTURE MEDITATION: *Live freely, animated and motivated by God's Spirit. Then you won't feed the compulsions of selfishness. For there is a root of sinful self-interest in us that is at odds with a free spirit, just as the free spirit is incompatible with selfishness. These two ways of life are antithetical, so that you cannot live at times one way and at times another way according to how you feel on any given day. Why don't you choose to be led by the Spirit and so escape the erratic compulsions of a law-dominated existence?* (Gal. 5:16–18 The Message).

45

THE SQUATTING, SMILING, INCARNATIONAL ARTIST

A poet is a man who not only suffers
the "impact of external events" but experiences
them . . . so that not only he, but we ourselves,
recognize that experience as our own.

—DOROTHY SAYERS

O ne of the most tantalizing wonders of the gospel is that Christ invaded our untidy existence and became one of us. "The Word became flesh and blood," says John, "and moved into the neighborhood" (John 1:14 *The Message*). He fully experienced the noisy block party of our existence: traffic jams, burnt toast, petty acquaintances, smelly feet, strep throat. Such a human picture flies in the face of the often-used term "spiritual." The word connotes a tranquil, ethereal, sanitary way of living.

A spiritual person seems like one who glides through life on a cushy cloud, spouting winsome words of wisdom and karma and leaving a sawdust trail-mix of glory behind. Somehow, it feels much tougher to think about Jesus *the person*. That's because the idea of a God who is like us in every substantive way is uncomfortable and unsettling. It means he does not stand aloof. It means he knows us to the gritty core.

One of the great temptations in any artistic venture is to distance ourselves, to withdraw from the messy world. There's no danger, no threat, when we can proclaim our artistic visions or lofty thoughts from the lectern of safety we often gain from the label of "artist." In fact, sometimes our protective pulpit of art actually prevents us from the dirty business of *living* what we create. "I think, therefore I am," the old adage goes. An apt paraphrase for the distanced artist would be, "I create, therefore I am."

But the incarnational act stops us frozen in our all-too-often undisturbed tracks. To be an artist, a Christ-ful artist, we are invited to resist the temptation to allow life to glance off us like a child's suction-cup arrow. Christ lovingly bids us to enter fully into the humdrum ordinariness of all-night fishing, the exuberant joy of wedding celebrations (topped off by the best wine available), the painful disappointment of friends abandoning us in our darkest hour. Because of his own life, he invites us to enter, as the poet Geoffrey Hill calls it, "our common, puddled substance."

The incarnational artist will find it impossible to be a bystander to life, or to use art as a means to distance himself or herself from anyone. Every meeting of hearts, chance or otherwise, is seen as a possibility for both unmitigated glory and gut-wrenching pain (consider dear C. S. Lewis and his one, great love, Joy). It is the gorgeous, humbling task of the incarnational artist to, in addition to his or her art, actually *become* the art created. In this way, those who enjoy our painting or teaching or needlepointing are so caught up, our art also becomes their art as well. Life becomes art, and then is turned back to life again—through the lives of those who taste the Artist.

The artist who, like Christ, fully "moves into the neighborhood" is the one who causes our hearts to burn within us. And the true glory of glory often presents itself as plain, white bread. Simple. Unadorned. Humbling. The lowly truth about the artist who is a pilgrim on the path toward heaven is that he or she is, first and foremost, the imitator of One who preferred to hang out with dysfunctional fishermen and slimy IRS agents. Anything less is not incarnational art; it's solipsistic snobbery.

The incarnational artist of the soul resists the strong temptation to fortress himself in the dreamy castle of pretentious illusion, where servant-patrons scurry around him wondering what grandiose banquet of ideas they could possibly offer . . . *the artist*. Instead, he lives smack in the middle of the beachfront of life, just as Jesus did—squatting, smiling, and frying up fish.

Even for his most creatively-challenged friends.

PRAYER: *Jesus, help me to fully move into the neighborhood I live in—and not miss the chance to serve up my art in everyday ways.*

46

LADIES AND GENTLEMEN, ARE THERE ANY QUESTIONS?

The greatest inspiration is often born of desperation.
—CORNER COTRELL

The literary works of Chaim Potok, author of *The Chosen* and *My Name is Asher Lev,* are steeped in his Hasidic Jewish heritage. In a newspaper interview several years ago, the novelist describes his typical main characters as kids who are both in love with their faith and, at the same time, "in love with things alien to their Jewishness in the secular, Western world." Potok's works explore the tension these young people face: How does one bridge the ever-widening gap between belief in God—and that God's relevance to modern culture?

The parents in Potok's novels are often influenced by Eastern European traditions and thought. Because of this, their means of expressing their faith—and struggling with it—are often different from that of their American contemporaries. For example, Potok says, there is a difference between how the two cultures deal with tragedy:

"A Jew will stand up in the synagogue in front of the Ark and scream to God. Here we don't do it because it's America and we're very polite. But in Europe, a woman who, God forbid, has just lost her son, would run into the synagogue, pull open the curtains of the Ark and scream at the Torah scroll, 'What did you do to me? What kind of God are you? How do you rule the world this way?' . . .

"And she would scream and yell and pour out her heart and rage at this God. She would never say there was no God."

For the European Jew, asking the hard questions was a matter of faith. It meant you truly believed. The worst thing in the world, Potok says, was simply assuming God didn't exist—and therefore, never asking.

We often don't like questions. We want answers. We want resolution. Especially when it comes to matters of faith. Giving the right answers is what we're created for, isn't it? After all, how solid is our belief if we don't have everything neatly solved?

Yet asking God the hard questions is an art of the soul—and it makes for good art as well.

Take the case of Job. Here was a man blessed with it all: a great investment portfolio, a dude ranch with plenty of maids and butlers, his own personal grazing and petting zoo, ten terrific kids, and excellent quality of life. He also was passionately devoted to God—continuously offering him beyond what was required. You've heard of someone "going the extra mile"? Well, Job walked ten—and it was probably uphill in the snow.

Then, suddenly, overnight—every joy vanished. Poof. A regular spiritual stock market crash. No more money, no servants, no animals, no kids, no health. If people were poems, Job is T. S. Eliot's *The Waste Land.* His soul's terrain was a gritty, arid prairie—filled with old, abandoned houses of memories and howling winds of doubt. He had nothing but questions, questions, questions for his God.

On her album *Turbulent Indigo,* Joni Mitchell poeticizes Job's existential-sounding anguish in words that might connect with some of our own life-experiences:

THE SIRE OF SORROW (JOB'S SAD SONG)

Let me speak, let me spit out my bitterness—
Born of grief and nights without sleep and festering flesh.
Do you have eyes?
Can you see like mankind sees?
Why have you soured and curdled me?
Oh you tireless watcher! What have I done to you?
That you make everything I dread and
everything I fear come true?

Once I was blessed, I was awaited like the rain,
Like eyes for the blind, like feet for the lame.
Kings heard my words, and they sought out my company.
But now the janitors of Shadowland flick their brooms at me.
Oh you tireless watcher! What have I done to you?
That you make everything I dread and
everything I fear come true? . . .

You might say Joni Mitchell's portrayal of Job looks at life from both sides now. During seasons of suffering, hard questions erupt in our souls like Job's painful sores. And often there aren't any answers, because we can't sneak a peek backstage at the grand drama unfolding in the heavens. In Job's situation, he had no clue that all his troubles were part of an elaborate bidding war between God and Satan. And even if he had, it's doubtful that knowing *why* would have relieved his personal grief. Nothing would have stopped his successive major-depressive episodes.

The problem faced by Chaim Potok's young protagonists is one we often encounter as artists of the soul: How do we artistically connect our belief in God with modern culture? Perhaps one answer is the fine art of asking hard questions. Daring to voice our shared questions as human beings can serve as an artistic bridge between the worlds of faith and doubt, between Christ and culture.

Just as Chaim Potok reflects about his Jewish heritage, our very act of questioning God assumes we believe there really is a God. Like Joni Mitchell's haunting song of Job's lament, the art that dares address God about the woes of the world professes belief in that very same God.

Any questions?

CREATIVE SPIRITUAL EXERCISE: *What are some of your more painful or confusing questions for God? Create a work of art this week that asks one of those questions.*

47

GRACIOUS REJECTION

> *The great American novel has not only*
> *already been written, it has already been rejected.*
>
> —FRANK DANE

The most artistic moments in the Bible are often the most gracious. And one such moment is a tearful reunion scene between a group of hopelessly estranged brothers.

You know the story: Joseph was dearly loved by his father, Jacob. And to express his paternal affection, Jacob had an ornamental robe made for his son—one that surely would've made Elton John's concert get-ups look conservative in comparison.

Joseph's brothers hated his guts. They were insanely jealous of this seventeen-year-old daddy's boy. And it didn't help that Joseph freely shared with them his frequent dreams that someday he would rule over them. How grandiose, they thought. Let's put an end to this superiority complex.

So, one day, the brothers successfully faked Joseph's death and sent their brother packing. Jacob's sons reveled that they'd finally rid themselves of the narcissistic dreamer for good. And for years it appeared they had, as Joseph faithfully apprenticed in the school of suffering.

But eventually, the truth blazing in Joseph's heart couldn't hide any longer. God's calling for Joseph emerged, just as silver-bright and whole-grained hopeful as he'd dreamed years before: Pharaoh appointed him as head of state of the entire land of Egypt.

Joseph used that creative dreaming talent of his on behalf of others. He diligently prepared the country for the coming seven years of famine by stockpiling food during the seven prosperous years before. So when the hard times hit and Joseph's brothers came to Egypt in desperate search of nourishment, Jacob's flamboyant-garbed son was good and ready for them. But not so his bodyguards could break their kneecaps.

When Joseph's brothers finally realized who he was, they were shocked and terrified. But Joseph surprised them by weeping over them and kissing them. He assured them, "Don't worry. What you meant for harm, God meant for good" (Gen. 45:5; 50:20). Joseph knew that all his prophetic dreams, all his dungeon hardships, all his unusual people skills were designed for one simple purpose: to rain God's grace on those he loved most in their darkest hour.

In the presence of holy art, such as Joseph's life, we can't help being humbled into gratitude. And gracious, grace-filled creativity is the calling of the artist of the soul.

Gracious creativity sees clearly the barren landscape of artistic famine and plans ahead to offer its richest gifts in the greatest hour of need. It uses every solitary moment spent in the dark, dank prison cells of the soul for the art of the future. It is unafraid to dream boldly and to look foolish in front of others, all for the sake of kingdom destiny. And it takes personal artistic rejection and turns it into an opportunity to bless those who don't have eyes to see.

Afraid to submit your short story, play, poem for publication? Like Joseph, gracious creativity moves forward through good times and bad, despite frequent rejection. Is your art called too strange, too novel, too cutting-edge for the circles you travel in? Like Joseph, be faithful to harvest its rich, going-against-the-grain goodness—and always be prepared to offer something fresh to your family.

For those who fear rejection, Joseph is our metaphor: God places us in our particular circumstances, with our particular talents, *to do good to others*. The next time you're hurt when someone breezily dismisses your latest oil painting, remind yourself of your sense of destiny: Remember that bright, colorful robe and shiny ring and fatted calf your Father gave you as a present when you stumbled back into his arms. You're his Joseph.

With a calling like that, you can afford to be gracious.

CREATIVE MEDITATION: *Julian of Norwich called Christ "the most courteous one." What do you think of when you hear the words "courteous" or "gracious"? Spend some time in contemplative prayer this week, focusing on this aspect of spiritual graciousness.*

48

LET ART RUN ITS COURSE

Art for art's sake is a philosophy of the well-fed.

—YU CAO

Folk singer and songwriter David Wilcox consistently delivers some of the best meals on wheels in the business. The troubadour travels from town to town, playing concerts, bars, coffeehouses, wherever—dishing up his unique flavor of musical poetry. And those familiar with his songs know they're poetry you chew reflectively, thoughtfully. Poetry you digest slowly. Poetry you savor—and then crave again. And again. To his hungry listeners, David Wilcox serves up the full meal deal every time.

Yet this musician doesn't broadcast his recipe. And that's what makes his lyrics so incredibly appetizing—both to spice-lovers who know exactly what they're inhaling and to those who wouldn't know thyme from mint and cumin. Come and dine, Wilcox smiles. No matter who you are. No matter what condition your taste buds are in.

Here's part of the lyrics of "Secret Church" from his 1997 album *Turning Point*:

This great cold steel
that bars the way inside
was molten when the blacksmith
was still living
This dead heavy door

that's oak by oak
and all the way across is unforgiving
The inscription tall
on that pristine wall
behind the steel so rusted
says "Love remains
to break the chains
of those who would dare to trust it."

Meet me here any night
There's a secret church
that's gathered
by these gates of steel
a gathering of refugees
enough to feel
that we're warm inside
with our candles in the wind
Though we're standing on the outside
of these walls alone
the secret church
feels taller than cathedral stone
The doors may be locked
but they're just doors
Come be welcomed
into so much more
Come be welcomed
into so much more . . .

Welcome—even if you feel locked out. There's a church, the
musician says, that operates outside these physical walls. Love

remains to break the chains of those who would dare to trust it. Come be welcomed into so much more. Come and dine.

Jesus was good at inviting people "into so much more." In fact, one of his best "welcome" stories of all comes straight from the smoky club scene of its day. In John 4, Jesus meets a modern-day bar-hopper—a Samaritan woman—at a well-known watering hole. He asks her for a drink of water. This was really something: In those days, Jews made sure they didn't even talk to Samaritans. (They probably didn't listen to their music or send their children to the same schools, either.) The woman is astounded—and interested.

She and Jesus have a nice neighborly chat. Sort of. Until the point in the conversation when Christ tells her to go get her husband and come back. When she denies having a husband, Jesus offers the picture-perfect, precise lyrics of God, tailor-made for this woman's soul:

"That's nicely put: 'I have no husband.' You've had five husbands, and the man you're living with now isn't even your husband. You spoke the truth there, sure enough" (vv. 17–18 *The Message*).

Very politely, Jesus tells this woman she's trailer trash. But she doesn't appear hurt by hearing the truth about her sleazy lifestyle. She knows Jesus must be a prophet of some sort—and immediately she asks the question that's really bugging her: "Am I going to have to worship at the same place you Jews do?" In other words, "Can I taste God in the bar I've been attending—or will I need to get a square meal from the Baptist church?"

But Jesus doesn't go in either direction. He says that soon she won't be worrying about worshiping at either the bar *or* the Baptist church: "But the time is coming—it has, in fact, come—when what you're called will not matter and where you go to worship will not matter.

"It's who you are and the way you live that count before God. Your worship must engage your spirit in the pursuit of truth. That's the kind of people the Father is out looking for: those who are simply and honestly *themselves* before him in their worship. God is sheer being itself—Spirit. Those who worship him must do it out of their very being, their spirits, their true selves, in adoration" (vv. 21–24 *The Message*).

Jesus tells this woman it's no longer important if someone calls her a Baptist or a bar-mitzvah hopper, because the labels aren't what matter. Then he unhinges the thick, heavy, oak doors that had once blocked this woman's entry into the kingdom. My church is no longer a physical location, he tells her. It's within the heart. Heart tied to heart. A church bigger than temple—or cathedral—stone.

But the Samaritan woman doesn't really get it.

What she does get, though, is that what Jesus told her pulled no punches. And how in the world did he know about her secret life? Christ confused her—and intrigued her. She went away from that well and told all her friends that they needed to come see this Jesus guy.

In concert. Next time he played a gig. Coffee bar or Baptist church—it didn't matter. She liked the music—and she didn't even know the lyrics yet.

Come and dine.

The people of God, the living body of Christ, are like the components of a fine meal. Every course is important; every course matters. And there's more to kingdom-cuisine than simply dishing up the main course inside church walls. Like the fine art of serving hors d'oeuvres.

Here's a toast to David Wilcox, a musician who knows how to create delicious poetic appetizers: The artist who most fully savors the banquet knows *every* course is a work of Art. Art for pure Art's sake—from the first, wilted spinach salad to that last, rich, long-awaited dessert.

The artist of the soul lets Art run its course. Wherever the course is served.

CREATIVE SPIRITUAL EXERCISE: *The Samaritans in your life are those whom you avoid because either their beliefs—or their morals—are different from yours. Jesus didn't first minister to the Samaritan woman—he needed something from her. He asked her for a drink of water. How about asking a Samaritan for help this week—something you need physically, emotionally, spiritually?*

49

ARE BONFIRES VANITIES?

Creativity is itself an act of optimism.

—EDWARD ALBEE

he playwright Edward Albee, author of *Who's Afraid of Virginia Woolf?*, reflects on a unique dream he once had: He was lying leisurely on the beach with several friends, gathered around a bonfire fueled by driftwood. Then, on the horizon, hundreds of miles away, he saw a huge, silent explosion of fire. East, west, north, south—on all sides, the fires began to blaze bright orange amid the black night. In the dream, Albee had no doubt about what he was seeing. He quietly accepted the fact that he was watching the world end, and that, in a matter of seconds, he and his friends would be gone forever.

Albee used to have that bonfire dream quite often—and he ended up using it as creative fodder. He felt it connected directly with risks he took in his writing: "I think the ability to visualize the end of the world is probably a constructive step," he says. "[Y]ou take a chance every time you write, you risk your psyche, your mind, and your career. But you've got to take chances to find out what's in your head."

Edward Albee's dream affected him in a manner reminiscent of the familiar Latin phrase *carpe diem*, or "seize the day." The playwright's image of the world's ending sparked his desire to risk more at all times—to find out what was still "in his head," begging to be written. Strangely, what some would call Albee's "vision of gloom" actually gave him creative room.

Nope—we're not going to talk about the end of the world here (even though it's a hot topic these days). We're actually going to talk about that word often dreaded by artists and artists of the soul alike: *discipline*. Discipline for our art—and our heart. The subject is as popular among certain creative types as a nuclear warhead. And, you may ask, what does discipline have to do with Edward Albee's bonfire dream? Hold onto your beach hat. We'll get through the cloud cover.

Artists who desire discipline walk a precarious path of hot coals—tiptoeing constantly between the temptations of complacency and urgency. On one hand, if you create only when the muse hits, you might lollygag endlessly on the bayou of your brain, waiting for inspiration to drop like fried catfish from the sky. On the other hand, if you grow too determined, too dogged, your art can radiate the urgent feel of an end-times, heat-seeking missile: By golly, nothing's going to get in its metallica-driven way. When it comes to discipline and art, you don't want to get lazy . . . but you also don't want to end up getting too intense. It's easy to feel swamped.

So how in the world do you catch the *carpe* in your *diem*?

Perhaps the middle ground of artistic discipline is found in "peaceful purposefulness": being restful but not complacent, directed but not driven. The artist's vision of peaceful purposefulness is best described by the apostle Peter, who writes, "As obedient children, let yourselves be pulled into a way of life shaped by God's life, a life energetic and blazing with holiness. God says, 'I am holy; you be holy.' You call out to God for help and he helps—he's a good Father that way. But don't forget, he's also a responsible Father, and won't let you get by with sloppy living" (1 Pet. 1:14–17 *The Message*).

Discipline? Let yourself be pulled into a rhythmic way of living and creating, the way a salty tide might gently tug you to shore. Let the light and life of God blaze on you and through the work of your hands, as clean as the noontime sun. And let your creative energy be fueled by the same energy that fuels the creativity of God: holiness. How, when, where you create—doesn't matter, really. Peaceful purposefulness.

Discipline? God is a good Father and delights in helping us to create good soul-art. And, like anyone with aesthetic sensibilities, he's not too impressed with haphazard, sloppy work. He's the kind of artist-mentor who brings out the best in our own work—the kind who both encourages us and yet sets a higher artistic standard for us to aim for. So live and create from this sort of motivation. Peaceful purposefulness.

Discipline? It bugs some people to hear talk about a God who requires responsibility, who both loves us and yet calls us to more. Those same people may also be disturbed by Edward Albee's doomsday bonfire dream. But then, what's important is how you look at it: The playwright's glimpse of life's end propelled him into living. And, in the art of the soul, the word "discipline" doesn't spell doom and gloom; it spells peace and purpose. It spells seize the day . . . God's way.

With apologies to Tom Wolfe: Bonfires aren't always vanities.

CREATIVE EXERCISE: *Use the "peaceful purposefulness" approach this week on a favorite art project . . . and see where it takes you.*

50

GIVE US THIS DAY
OUR WONDER BREAD

Do we need miracles or do we need
only to perceive that every ordinary thing
around us is already miraculous?

—ELIZABETH ROONEY

S implicity is an art. Sometimes a cold glass of water, a steaming hot bowl of vegetable soup, a hunk of warm, brown bread is the most lovely, comforting thing of all. And artists—including artists of the soul—who offer us the gift of simplicity often grace us with our brightest glimpses of God.

The poet Elizabeth Rooney was one of those rare artists—a woman who lived, prayed, and wrote with a keen sense of wonder in the ordinary. Her poetry grounded in a "practical earthiness," a rich awareness of everyday marvels. And writing poetry itself was, for her, a marvel.

In 1978, while being inducted into a lay order of Episcopal women, the Society of the Companions of the Holy Cross, Elizabeth experienced the Holy Spirit's presence in a remarkable way. "I fell in love with God," she says. "It was as if my veins were bubbling with champagne." Even though she held a master's degree in Christian Education from Columbia University and Union Theological Seminary—studying under such theologians as Niebuhr and Tillich—nothing had prepared Elizabeth for this sudden sense of joy and intimacy with God. Of her seminary training she says, "I always felt like we were learning about God as if we were learning about algebra." Now she had encountered a living Word.

One of the results of Elizabeth's experience with the Word was that she was given the gift of words. In a letter to a friend, she describes the works' arrival as being delicate butterflies: "I try to net them and get them on paper without knocking too many bright bits of color off their wings." For the rest of Elizabeth's life, poetry's gossamer wings brushed her soul with shades of shimmering beauty.

Elizabeth lived most of her life at her family's farm in Blue Mounds, Wisconsin—a farm situated above an underground cave tourist site. Her love of the earth steeped her writing in the metaphors of the natural world: sweeping wild geese, trees aflame with a holy, burning presence. Many of her poems are simple prayers, or brief descriptions of quiet moments with God:

PRACTICE OF THE PRESENCE

The brightness burns
Along the brittle bone.
Heart-haunted,
I am jolted by the thud
Of Love along my veins.
Flesh turns translucent.
Mind-abashed,
Resigns its tyranny
And only God remains.

Elizabeth Rooney went home recently to sit face-to-face with that Love she so craved to touch in this life. But she left behind a spiritual legacy through her journals and poetry—a legacy bright and hauntingly simple. In a manuscript yet unpublished, she offers the well-worn wisdom and beauty of her everyday heart:

"There's a moment after a party when the last dish is put away, the house is silent and shining, the refrigerator is full of unaccustomed goodies, my mind is full of scraps of conversation, bits of laughter and good moments, the daily routine has not yet reasserted itself and content fills me.

"I sat on the porch and wondered about the kind of God who made water into wine in Cana of Galilee so that the father of the bride would not suffer a social disaster; a disgrace, however minor. Does God really care about our parties being successful? Apparently, He does. How infinitely loving of Him!"

God of grace, please give us this day our wonder bread.

CREATIVE MEDITATION
(FROM ELIZABETH ROONEY'S JOURNAL):

FISH WIFE

Can you use a fish wife, Lord?
My face, seamed with the sun,
My feet, splayed,
And my arms like shrunken rope?
My voice is harsh, Lord,
My speech is sharper than salt.
I smell of bilge water and brine.

Peace, woman!
Have you forgotten how it began,
How, long ago,
I made friends with a fisherman?

51

IMAGINE FAITH'S HOPE

Imagination decides everything.

—BLAISE PASCAL

he painter Marc Chagall's work (1887–1985) is recognized for both its playful, uninhibited use of color and its primitive styles. Chagall's passionate portrayals of life are exuberantly evident in such paintings as *The Blue Circus, Peasant Life,* and *The Fiddler*—portrayals that mirror our shared longing for joy, for bliss. His human figures often float in midair. As Sister Wendy Beckett says of Chagall, "At heart he was a religious painter, using the word in its widest sense: he painted the dreams of the heart, not the mind, and his fantasy is never fantastic."

Those are intriguing words, Sister Wendy: Fantasy that is not fantastic. In the art world, what does that mean? What's the difference between the two? And for that matter, what's the difference between unhealthy fantasy and healthy imagination?

One resource for exploring these mysteries is the work of American Jesuit William F. Lynch, S.J. Lynch spent a lifetime pondering the role of imagination in the faith-life, the connections between art and belief. For him, faith was the imagination that births images—images that later become the vehicles for how that belief is lived out. Faith grants us images that remind us of the reality of God.

Lynch's thoughts were influenced by those of the philosopher Friederich Schelling. Schelling believed humans use three separate levels of imaginative process: The *ursprungliche Anschauung,* or passive imagination, which absorbs; the active imagination, *Einbuidungskraft,* which organizes; and the *Kunstvermogen,* the creative imagination, which finds expression. Since nature gives tactile expression to God's imagination, our human artistic expressions mirror that imagination. Schelling saw imagination as the one thing that set people free from themselves and helped them to vigorously enter their world. In this way, he mused, the imagination was a form of love.

When we speak of fantasy, we speak of imagination—in its best and truest sense. Most of us can't help thinking of certain literary works that, in some ways, define fantasy—hallmark books that have been staples on our bookshelves for a lifetime: Lewis's *Perelandra,* Tolkien's *Lord of the Rings.* Reflecting on the longevity and enduring appeal of these works might help us to wade through distinguishing unhealthy fantasy—or the illusionary fantastic—from imagination.

Lynch's idea—that faith grants us images that remind us of God—is a liberating concept for the artist of the soul. Artists are notorious for "flights of fantasy"—or mistakenly seen as those who board that plane of existence regularly. As one artist friend confided, "My non-artist friends often view me as someone who's just out to 'do my own thing'—no accountability, wriggling to get out of the church's confines." Her struggle is common: The artist's life is often a frustrating, lonely experience—because those who don't choose to use their imaginations often mistake the visionary imagination for the illusionary fantastic. Or, as William Lynch might say, they mistake unhealthy fantasy with the reality of faith.

Here are just a few thoughts on this subject I'm muddling around with myself. Feel free to pick and choose what you'd like:

- Perhaps the fantastic is an escape from the reality of ourselves, our true nature—while imagination is a journey deeper into ourselves, in a way that more intimately connects us with God and others.

- The fantastic twists and turns until it ends in illegitimate satisfaction; imagination twists and turns, only to lead us to more truthful twists and turns.

- The fantastic is the illusion of imagination; imagination travels beyond trite illusion—and enters into the realm of faith.

Perhaps there's no greater illusion than believing you possess faith—when in reality you are living with a hardened, calcified imagination. If faith, hope, and love are connected to one another, then faith—your ability to trust what you cannot see—ties directly into your ability to hope. Healthy fantasy leads to hope's glimmers; the unhealthy fantastic leads to cynicism's surety.

If imagination is a form of love, as Schelling believed, then artists are the ones who should most resemble Jesus. And those who look like Jesus love and serve and give as he did.

And he did so every day among a people with no "ears to hear and eyes to see." A people with absolutely no imagination. Let us go out and do likewise.

Imagine faith's hope. It's nothing but fantasy . . . in the best sense of the word.

SCRIPTURE MEDITATION: *Now faith is the substance of things hoped for, the evidence of things not seen. This is what the ancients were commended for* (Heb. 11:1–2).

52

HOW THE SPIKE
GOT HIS PUNCH

> *It seems safe to say that significant discovery,*
> *really creative thinking, does not occur with regard to*
> *problems about which the thinker is lukewarm.*
>
> —MARY HENLE

*I*f you've seen more than one Spike Lee movie, you know there's a little "film doohickie" the filmmaker often pulls on the audience. Just when you're engrossed in the story, the director places one of the characters on an unseen dolly that begins moving as the character speaks. The effect breaks the plane of disbelief; it's as if the filmmaker looks directly into the camera at you and says, "Hey guys, this is only a movie." You sort of laugh to yourself, shift in your seat, think, "Yeah, here we go. There's that Spike-move again."

Yet, at the same time, the filmmaker uses this predictable style-effect to invade your personal space. Now Spike himself is sitting right next to you, munching popcorn, commenting on, laughing at his own movie. And we have to look at the movie through his eyes, not just our own. Spike's joke-technique often creates a response that's the exact opposite of your first reaction: This *isn't* just a movie. There's something about the reality of the African-American experience that the filmmaker wants to make sure we get—and get good.

Spike Lee's filmmaking idiosyncrasies aren't just stylistic embellishments; the director is very intentional with his artistic expression. That's because the uniqueness of his work is secondary to his passion in communicating his message. In other words, when you leave one of his films, you're not thinking about his familiar dolly-move. You're thinking about the fervent beliefs of Malcolm X or the shattered dreams of urban youth. Lee's films are driven consistently by the most important thing in any creative work:

Passion is its name.

And if you got it, then you got game.

In the book of Revelation, when the apostle John is instructed to write the message of Christ to the seven churches, the hardest and most painful words are left for last (3:14–21). They are written to the church in Laodicea, whose deeds were neither hot nor cold—but lukewarm. He tells them that, even though they think they're incredibly rich in every possible way, in reality they're poor, blind, naked. Tepid as day-old bahwater. Even though the other churches John wrote to had committed all manner of evil, God was most grieved by the people who would neither fervently reject him nor embrace him. He wanted passion. He wanted their white-hot love for him, a lightning-love that consumed all other loves and wants.

As artists, when we're illegitimately "rich," as the church in Laodicea was, we think we're creating art that's unique and wonderful. But in reality it's dead and lifeless. Why? *The work of art that makes uniqueness its goal has already failed.* It's lukewarm art. And the lukewarm artist is one whose pursuit of uniqueness has left his soul tepid.

This sort of art is characterized by the meandering, so-what pursuit to create something, anything that will buy our way out of the art-ghetto. Yet whenever we sell our souls simply for the sake of being different, we become artistically poor, blind, naked—stripped of the blazing life-force that fuels creativity. We are stripped of our passion for Art.

Artists of the soul aren't lukewarm about *anything*—most importantly the truth. And the most important aspect to creating works of art—and living an artful life—isn't trying to be unique or different; it's being passionate. Passionate about what you believe, care about, hope for. If you live and love passionately, then what is most unique about your own soul will automatically spring to life and flourish—sprouting wildly among the wilted, tired weeds of the world.

Like Spike Lee, you're already a one-of-a-kind artist—with your own styles, tastes, quirks, trademarks. After all, you're made in the image of a God who's anything but generic.

Be passionate about what you believe and the rest will take care of itself.

Or, as the filmmaker would say, just do the right thing.

CREATIVE MEDITATION: *We can only serve God with burning love, with complete devotion of time and energy, with willingness to sacrifice and with a fervent heart.*

—BASILEA SCHLINK

SOURCES

3. Art? What a Waste...: John Green, "The Underground Life of a
    Russian Intellectual," *Detroit News* (April 28, 1974); Tom Asick,
    "Muggeridge on Critics, Christianity," *Washington Star-News*
    (February 18, 1975).
4. Einstein's Genius: Jerome Weidman, "How I Learned to Listen,"
    Musical Gems from the Reader's Digest (Pleasantville. Reader's Digest
    Association, 1961), 7–13.
6. Seeing in Black and White: David Bremer and Ched Myers, "The
    Flutter of History: Wim Wenders' film view of angels in our midst,"
    Sojourners (July 1994). Interview with Wim Wenders, back cover of
    sleeve of the NTSC Laserdisc release of *Faraway, So Close.*
8. Playing by Bill Romanowski's Rules: Carl Jung as quoted in
    Christopher Bryant, *Jung and the Christian Way* (London: Darton,
    Longman, and Todd, 1983), 70.
10. There Goes Art...Acting Up Again: *The Norton Anthology of Literature
    by Women,* Ed. Sandra M. Gilbert and Susan Gubar (New York:
    W.W. Norton), 1852–1854. Kathleen Raine, *The Inner Journey of the
    Poet* (New York: George Braziller, 1982), 32.
11. We're All a Bunch of Marthas: Gene Edward Veith, Jr., *Postmodern
    Times: A Christian Guide to Contemporary Thought and Culture*
    (Wheaton, Ill: Crossway Books, 1994), 115.
12. Scarred for Life: Greg Wakowsky, "The Realism of Recovery,"
    Christianity and the Arts, 6, no. 3 (Summer 1999), 13–15. Rick
    Lyman, "Vassar Miller, 74, Texas Poet; Her Infirmity Inspired Her
    Art," *New York Times,* November, 1998.
16. I Love to Tell the Story: Margaret Guenther, *Holy Listening: The Art of
    Spiritual Direction* (Cambridge and Boston: Cowley Publications, 1992);
    Andrew Murray, *Humility* (Grand Rapids: Zondervan, 1988), 44.
19. How to be "Low Man" on the Totem Pole: John Lahr, "Making
    Willy Loman," *The New Yorker* (January 25, 1999), 42–49; Jay Carr,

"Arthur Miller Sheds Light on 'Salesman'" *Detroit News* (November 25, 1973); James Wesley Ingles, "Realism in Christian Writing," in *The Christian Imagination: Essays on Literature and the Arts,* ed. Leland Ryken (Grand Rapids: Baker Book House, 1981), 341.

20. Orchestrating a Blind Date: Nancy Franklin, "A master and maverick make beautiful music together," *New Yorker* (October 19, 1998), 28-29.

21. A Classic Case: David Denby, *Great Books: My Adventures with Homer, Rousseau, Woolf, and Other Indestructible Writers of the Western World* (New York: Simon & Schuster, 1996), 11–15, 177, 238.

22. "And the Oscar for Best Disciple in a Supporting Role Goes to…": Anna C. Krausse, *The Story of Painting: From the Renaissance to the Present* (Koin: Konemann, 1995), 15.

23. Playing Musical Chores: "Harold C. Schonberg, "Tyrants—and Gods—of the Podium," *Musical Gems from the* Reader's Digest, (Pleasantville: Reader's Digest Association, 1961), 122.

24. When God Throws the Book at You: Richard Corliss, "Dazzling Decalogue," *Time* (July 27, 1998), 61.

26. Obviously: Order from Bizzell Bookcovers, N4U2 Unlimited, 104 N. Scott Road, Poteau, OK 74953.

27. And the Beat Goes On…: Howard Gardner, *Creating Minds: An Anatomy of Creativity Seen Through the Minds of Freud, Einstein, Picasso, Stravinsky, Eliot, Graham, and Gandhi* (New York: Basic Books, 1993), 280.

28. Cross Purposes: Francois Truffaut, tr. Leonard Mayhew, *The Films in My Life* (New York: Da Copa Press, 1994), 1, 34–35.

29. Processing Food: M.F.K. Fisher, "Love in a Dish," *House Beautiful* (March 1996), 80–82, 148.

30. The Hidden Chambers of Art: David McCasland, *Oswald Chambers: Abandoned to God* (Grand Rapids: Discovery House, 1993), 40–42, 158–59.

31. Beauty's Prayer: David Lehman, *The Last Avant-Garde: The Making of the New York School of Poets* (New York: Doubleday, 1998), 25.

34. Dragging One Another Through the Mud: J. M Thornburn, as quoted by Margaret Miles in *Context* "Martin E. Marty on Religion and Culture," 30, no. 2 (January 15, 1998).

35. Perspectives on Popeye: Anna C. Krausse, *The Story of Painting: From the Renaissance to the Present* (Koin: Konemann, 1995), 7

38. Baby Steps: R. G. Collingwood, "Making and Creation," in *Creativity in the Arts,* ed. Vincent Tomas (Prentice-Hall, Inc.: Englewood Cliffs, NJ, 1964), 7. Annie Dillard, "To Fashion a Text," from *Inventing the Truth: The Art and Craft of Memoir* (New York and Boston: Houghton Mifflin Company), 59.

40. Christ, Our Vanishing Point: Anna C. Krausse, *The Story of Painting: From the Renaissance to the Present* (Koin: Konemann, 1995), 9.

41. Metaphorically Speaking...: Gene Edward Veith, Jr., "Get Real," in *World* 13, no. 26 (July 4, 1998). Larry Woiwode, "The Word Made Flesh," *Books & Culture* (July-August, 1999), 39–41.

43. A Detailed, Itemized Statement: Barbara Nachman, "Designer defines 'standout': Flair apparent in home decor," *Denver Post* (July 31, 1999), 8F.

46. Ladies and Gentlemen, Are There Any Questions? Elizabeth Duff, "Chaim Potok: A writer caught between 2 cultures," *Philadelphia Enquirer* (April 27, 1976).

49. Are Bonfires Vanities? *Pittsburgh Press* (February 3, 1974).

50. Give Us This Day Our Wonder Bread: Luci Shaw, "Elizabeth Rooney," in *Meet the Men and Women We Call Heroes,* ed. Ann Spangler and Charles Turner (Ann Arbor: Servant Publications, 1985), 89–111. For more information on Elizabeth Rooney's work, see contact information in the permissions section of this book.

51.   Imagine Faith's Hope: Sister Wendy Beckett, *The Story of Painting: The Essential Guide to the History of Western Art* (London: Dorling Kindersley, 1994), 345; Gerald J. Bednar, *Faith as Imagination: The Contribution of William F. Lynch, S.J.* (Kansas City: Sheed & Ward, 1996), 138, 168.

Permissions